Women
mind your money
before someone else does

Gayle McKew

National Library of Australia Cataloguing-in-Publication entry (pbk)

Author:	McKew, Gayle, author.
Editor:	W Millgate, Wendy & Words
Title:	Women mind your money: before someone else does/ Gayle McKew
ISBN:	9780992453732 (paperback)
Subjects:	Women--Australia--Finance, Personal development.
Dewey Number:	332.024

Published by Gayle McKew and InHouse Publishing
www.inhousepublishing.com.au

Printed using Envirocare paper.

Disclaimer

Preparer: This document has been prepared by Gayle McKew, an Authorised Representative of HNW Planning Pty Ltd, AFSL 225216 (HNW) as at 16 May 2015.

General advice warning: The information contained in this document is general information only. It has been prepared without taking into account any person's specific financial situation, objectives or needs. The appropriateness of this information needs to be considered in that context.

Not an offer: This document is not an offer to issue any financial product—no part of the document is to be construed as solicitation or recommendation to make a financial investment. In no circumstances is the information in this document to be used by, or presented to, a person for the purposes of making a decision about a financial product or class of products.

No advice or verification: This document does not constitute personal financial or taxation advice. The material in this document has been prepared in good faith with all reasonable care. However, certain parts of this material are obtained or are based upon information obtained from third parties which may not have been checked or verified. Subsequent changes in circumstances may also occur at any time and may impact on the accuracy of the information.

Domicile of Information: This document has been prepared based on the writer's knowledge and interpretation of the Australian investment environment and legal advice the writer has previously paid for for her personal use. In no circumstances is the information in this document to be used by, or presented to, a person for the purposes of making a decision about a financial product, class of products or legal matters. Information provided is a guideline only. We strongly recommend you seek personal legal and or financial advice relative to your specific situation.

Foreword

Our finances are one of the major drivers of lifestyle and attitude. Along with health, they impact our view of the world and the way we meet the challenges we face each day.

Unfortunately, we are not taught the vagaries of savings, investments, insurance and retirement at school, and unless we are instructed by our parents, we are left to our own devices to search out advice and how that advice is applicable to our own situation, both now and in the future.

The television has become our financial planner and our mentor. The overwhelming volume of information overload available on the internet serves only to confuse; hence, nothing gets done until too late.

Gayle has done a fine job of breaking down the eternal mystery—where does all my money go? This book shows us how to break through the myths, take control of our finances, as it is only us who are ultimately responsible for our own lives, and take advantage of opportunities as they come our way.

I recommend this book as a map for anyone who wants to win back control of their finances.

Michael J Hanley Adv. Dip FP. Dip AII

Preface

Many people consider they are managing their money quite well if they are paying their rent and bills and putting food on the table, even though they are often not getting ahead. Others think because they have a house and mortgage things are good. But are they?

I, too, once measured success as owning a home. At 27, I blithely thought owning our home was *the* key to financial security and I should do absolutely nothing that could possibly put it at 'risk'. How wrong that thought process turned out to be…

Years ago my husband told me he wanted to invest $100 000 in a company in which we would have no control or input. Instead of asking for more information so I could understand the risks that might be involved, I pandered to the fear of losing our home. To invest, we would have had to borrow the whole amount against our home. My fear of 'what if' something went wrong kicked into overdrive! What I imagined at the time to be our security was disappearing before my very eyes. Blindly and fearfully, I said no to the opportunity without asking for more details or even seeking clarification. I'm not proud to say that that 'no' turned out to be *the* most expensive mistake I have ever made! Three years later, the very same business in which we were offered shares sold to a global buyer and every $100 000 investment turned into in excess of $1 million. Oops!

By saying 'no' to the opportunity, I've come to realise I was repelling what the Universe was trying to deliver. Silly mistake! Pandering to my fears had cost us in regard to lost opportunity *and* in actual dollar terms. My fear had pretty much sabotaged our future financial security. By being too afraid to ask questions I had been unable to identify the opportunity for what it was. I soon came to realise there is potentially as big a risk in playing it safe as there is in throwing caution to the wind when making decisions, particularly when it comes to investment decisions.

Living in fear of 'what if' comes with a cost. The costs can be important things like self-belief and focus and, of course, there is always the financial cost of playing it too safe. The lesson I got from my 'mistake' turned out to be priceless. It was the best 'mistake' of my life! I quickly set about learning how *not* to make similar errors of judgement again. If only I'd known the concept of *risk and reward* before making my decision, the outcome would have been so very different. That's 20/20 hindsight talking!

Let's be clear; when I talk of my 'mistake' I'm really referring to a major turning point. It was the start of a huge learning curve, creating an opportunity to learn, to reassess decision making processes and the start of taking measured risks. My 'mistake' was a positive starting point for creating the future. I became keen to learn everything about the world of finances, only to discover that the more I learnt the more there was to learn.

Some lessons were learnt as a result of personal mistakes, and others from direct exposure to a range of different businesses and becoming aware of their 'ethical' practices. Yet other lessons were from witnessing the impact of individual greed, which often resulted in significant financial and emotional impacts on individuals.

As a result of all I've seen and experienced, I can understand why people have trouble trusting my industry. Add to that the image of financial advisors portrayed by the media, which is often fear-mongering and widely damaging. Sadly, the media never tells of ethical practitioners who work with, and for, their clients' best interests.

I've advised people through good times and bad. During the fallout of the Global Financial Crisis (GFC), clients had my private, unlisted phone number. I took calls on my days off. For me, a client having peace of mind is worth far more than having an uninterrupted day off. Clients still have my number and know they can call any time with their concerns. But I can only take so many calls a day, which is one reason for writing this book.

It seemed even more important to share what I know when I began discovering how friends had made expensive mistakes, some of which caused the family home to be repossessed by the bank. One friend had been too embarrassed by the situation in which she found herself to reach out for help.

Stories like this made me realise there is a huge gap between what most people know and what they could benefit from knowing. While I take for granted the financial knowledge I have acquired over the years, other women are frequently financially ill-prepared, often through no fault of their own. Lack of awareness and options are evident. Lack of information and opportunity is as important as a lack of self-belief and action. People's values and mindset around money often appears not to be serving them well; the gap needs to be filled.

The overriding goal of *Women Mind Your Money* is for you to win back control over the way you manage your finances, so you don't have to make expensive financial and emotional mistakes. I want you to be in a position to make powerful decisions that will create the reality you dream of, instead of simply getting by using sheer dumb luck—you know, unintentionally and without planning.

I'm bringing to this money empowerment party a wealth of knowledge built up over more than 35 years working in financial services, studying and learning the ropes as I went along and making my own expensive errors along the way.

I started at the bottom and progressed as I learned. Eventually, I managed financial planning practices until deciding to become my own boss. I can now help people in the manner I feel is in *their* best interests. Because there's always something changing in this industry, I never stop learning, so I can add to my bag of tricks to be of value to my clients.

My personal mindset, thinking processes and actions have not always been mainstream. Many, many times I've been called a 'hippy'. My 'hippiness' (a quote from my son) has caused me to take on interesting beliefs and values with regard to money that are quite contrary to the traditional thinking of a financial planner. I understand money isn't meant to be held close to you and hoarded, as it will stifle the energy of the Universe; it's meant to be shared with everyone for the benefit of all as a great energetic flow. My dad used to say, 'Money's made round to go round', which pretty much sums it up in an 'old school' way. I don't mean you're to give everything away willy-nilly or not accrue wealth. But stick with me and you'll learn some new strategies that will make sense in the end, and will positively impact the way you see and use money.

Helping you gain some independence will give me a real buzz. I thrive on empowering others to be the best version of who they can be—to be masters of their own life. Let me guide you through the financial maze and provide clarity while unravelling and removing confusion and any blockages to financial success in your life. It *is* possible to plan for prosperity and achieve it. So jump on board as you learn to *Mind Your Money ... Before Someone Else Does* and get it working for you!

Gayle

Contents

As circumstances change, it's possible what you were told in the past will no longer hold true. Regularly reviewing what you've been told could provide you with an advantage. It doesn't always pay to believe everything you're told.

—*Gayle McKew*

Introduction

'If a man empties his purse into his head, no one can take it away from him. An investment in knowledge always pays the best interest.'
—Benjamin Franklin

You are holding the knowledge and tools to take back control of your finances; you can create the life you dream of. Once you have the know-how it's empowering to make decisions from a point of knowledge, where decisions and actions are yours. This is the gateway to independence.

How many times have you heard someone say 'I wish I knew then what I know now'? I've said this myself! Having the access to someone's hard-earned knowledge and experience, without having to make the errors, could make things so much easier. I wish someone had helped me *before* I made so many costly and time-consuming errors of my own!

Rather than make you do the hard yards, I'm pleased to share a little of that knowledge in *Women Mind Your Money.* I'm giving back.

Regardless of your relationship status there's something for you. Relationships bring financial and emotional impacts—some good, some difficult. Regardless of your situation, let's get you in charge so you can begin making powerful decisions for your future.

If you struggle to make ends meet, discover why you might be stuck in a negative cycle; learn to take control. This book is designed to deliver results. It will, if you commit to your future.

For those with good money skills already, discover even more information on money and protection, with great ways to protect your ass-ets (that's not a typo!). For the 'hippy' at heart there's even stuff on Universal Laws to attract the abundance you seek.

If you're already working with Universal Laws and not getting the results you'd like, the missing ingredient could be in your hands. Think financial information overlayed by spiritual 'stuff'. This book might provide the breakthrough needed to handle your money and create a degree of security for your future. It's certainly worth giving it a go!

This book is not simply a compilation of facts and figures; it's a melding of practical tips with words of encouragement and wisdom for everyone. Are you getting the results you dream of? Part of the problem could be that you are giving the Universe mixed messages.

Real-life stories are used to share core lessons and knowledge. Stories are the easiest way to illustrate how to harness the information to your advantage.

Mind Your Money at a glance

The beginning of this book, called *Foundation: Financial Check-up,* is *super* important to your success; it's an initial diagnosis of your situation. You need to know how much is coming in and going out, and if there's any leftover. If you already have a budget, you realise the importance of controlling cash flow.

You may have heard 'cash is king'; let's change this to 'cash-flow is queen'—as this is a book for women. As queen of your realm it is up to you to rule! It's time to change how you 'do' money.

Part 1 is all about getting your head in the game. Firstly, you will discover in *Your Money Relationship* what drives your actions and reality. Your beliefs may unconsciously be driving your decisions and habits.

Without a change in your thinking, nothing is going to work. Successful people know results are directly linked to what is happening in the mind!

In *Money Mindset Makeover* you will sort out ill-fitting beliefs and learn positive techniques to get money flowing. You deserve to achieve your goals and dreams; learn to tell the Universe what that life looks like.

In *Take Control*, we look at replacing old habits and how to build new, positive, practical strategies. There is always a way forward; you have to try something different until you begin to achieve success. If you stick to the path, you can develop skills to help negotiate marketing minefields created by modern retailers. Knowledge will position you with those marketing messages.

Uber-successful people do things differently; they *Think, Plan & Walk Like an Entrepreneur (Chapter 4).* Learn to take emotion out of decision making. Explore processes for success and how to benefit from managing money.

Part 2 is about really getting down to taking care of business. In *Good Debt-Bad Debt* discover the differences between good debt and bad and learn strategies to help manage debts and to understand how too much of the wrong debt could be sabotaging your success.

Loans and Leverage is about finding the best borrowing option for you and to understand the power and risk of leverage. And getting a loan won't be on the cards if you don't learn to protect *Your Credit Rating.* Consider in this chapter some things necessary to ensure you're able to protect yourself from damaging your financial future. Understanding what not to do is as important as knowing what to do to improve your financial future.

Part 3 focusses on how to protect yourself financially. *Relationship STDs* is all about protection, for you, now and in the future, regarding any relationship that you are in or about to step into.

In *Cover Your Financial Butt* we look at the importance of insurance; protecting yourself and your family.

Part 4 focuses on income and savings and begins with *Creating Extra Income Streams*. Here we discuss options to help you create powerful choices for the future. Imagine the lifestyle to be gained by having extra money to fund your choices!

Do you look forward to holidays? Have you started planning for *Your Longest Holiday* yet? Most people never plan past the short term. But if you start planning now you'll end up with many more opportunities to maintain or even boost your lifestyle.

Effective Estate Planning is often overlooked but not here. We need to make sure we prepare for eventual reality.

Finally, *Create a Master Plan* aims to provide some of the steps required to take your life forward. How many times have you had someone at a barbeque advise you to do something? I've given up counting how many times I've been told to do something that wasn't right for me! *Who's Your Adviser* is important; it filters out would-be advisers from real advisers.

* * *

There's a whole other world of opportunity to take advantage of, and I encourage you to keep reading, to take advantage of what I've learned. There's enough abundance for us all.

Take control of your finances; break through any financial chaos to create powerful alternatives and opportunities.

A word of warning ... It may seem I have two personalities—one a bit ethereal and dreamy; the other where I turn into a bit of a drill sergeant, wanting you to change habits and say 'No!' A relationship with money has many faces. I may need to be direct to cater to your inner child that's telling you to take no notice—that you can't do it! I'm here to say you can! Other times I might have my cranky pants on. This is because the subject is important to your success.

By progressing through this book, you're effectively implementing a major review of your financial operating system so your operating system works effectively *for you*. You see, my aim is to put *you in control* of your financial situation. The execution and success of your financial journey is entirely up to you. It takes time to form new habits and to undo those hurting you. I encourage you to value yourself and your dreams—you deserve it! I am absolutely passionate about your financial success, and you *need* to be too. In the end *you* are the controller of your future; it's time to gain mastery over that important part of your life. Are you ready to get started?

Remember, knowledge is the key to creating power. As we progress you should become clearer and much less stressed! It's time to understand your financial position now; know what you own and what you owe, through a *financial check-up*, which will provide you with a starting point to measure progress against in the future.

Foundation

Financial Check-Up

'A budget is telling your money where to go instead of wondering where it went.'

—Dave Ramsey[1]

Imagine you're not well and you don't know what's wrong. You can't even begin to fathom how to get better. If you do nothing, things will most likely get worse—especially if you worry! You go to the doctor who asks, 'Have you had a check-up recently?' They may order a barrage of tests to find out what's really going on. Based on the results, you may receive advice on how to improve things, which you will do your best to implement. Good on you!

Do you value your hard-earned money? How long has it been since your finances had a check-up? Have you *ever* checked where your finances are at? Without checking on your health your doctor wouldn't know how to improve and optimise your health. Your finances deserve similar treatment; it's time for a financial check-up to see where things are at.

By this I don't mean the last time you checked your account balance to see how much money you had left to spend or, worse yet, how much available credit was left on your credit card. That way of thinking is operating in survival mode and will be leading you towards disaster.

1 www.goodreads.com/quotes/349829-a-budget-is-telling-your-money-where-to-go-instead

There's nothing deliberate and powerful in that way of managing your money.

By a financial check-up I mean the last time you really looked at:

* how much you earn (after tax)
* how much you spend
* where your money goes—loans, lifestyle etc.
* if there is money left over at the end of each pay period
* if you have personal debt and no assets to show for it.

Experience shows most people never check their finances in this much detail. Instead, they get by without understanding what's happening with their money. They could, with a little effort, potentially get much better results.

Current strategies might mean your personal finances are either on life support or heading towards the emergency room in need of some serious resuscitation. Are you stumbling along without even knowing the state of your financial health? You and your future deserve more attention! Pull off the blinkers and take a long, hard look at the current state of your finances. The best way is through creating and sticking to a budget.

Budget is not a dirty word

I can hear some of you now thinking: *I don't have a budget. I don't need a budget. I don't want a budget. I suck at budgets!* I understand. Many of us think a budget is something to be avoided at all costs; it truly is a dirty word according to some people. It can be plain boring. Yet having a budget does have its benefits and is a crucial step towards financial freedom.

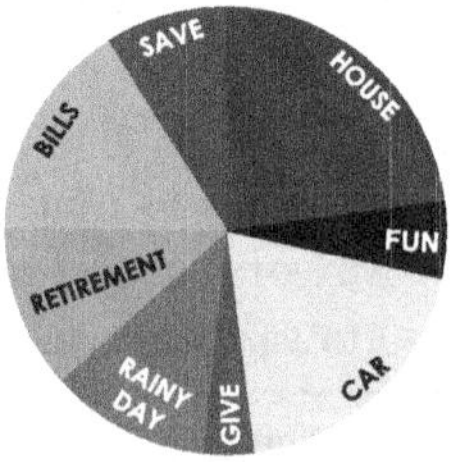

A budget is simply a written summary of your most likely income and expenses over a specific period of time.

The language of a budget is numbers, so for some it might be time to start learning a second language! I promise—it's not that hard. A budget will help you plan how to spend your money and pay bills. The pie chart shows this quite well; a budget is about identifying where you need to apply your money. Another way is to think of a pie—make sure every part of your life in need of money gets its fair 'slice' of your income pie.

Rather than simply focusing on paying bills, a good budget needs to be extremely wide-ranging as well as versatile. It needs to incorporate a plan for your future, as well as meet today's need for security. A good budget needs the basics plus generosity and a touch of creativity.

Make provision for things like giving to charities and for gifts to family and friends (Christmas and birthdays). Sprinkle in an allowance for enjoyment and fun things like annual holidays. Plan for a cash reserve and an emergency fund, just in case something goes wrong and it's required.

To be really successful, your budget will need to incorporate flexibility and yet have a good degree of structure built into it; it can't be haphazard in any way . It's that simple.

You know how much your pay cheque is going to be and where it's going to come from this week. Yet without a budget, will you know where you need to spend your money and how much will be left over to help you achieve your short- and long-term goals? You won't have a clue, or at best you'll be guessing. *Guessing is simply not an option* if you plan to succeed.

If you intend becoming wealthy or even comfortable in the future, you need to have a plan to follow as to how you spend and save your money. A budget is the beginning of your journey to a sound financial future.

A budget is the beginning of your journey to a sound financial future.

An added benefit of creating and working with a budget is you avoid paying late fees. Avoiding late fees means you keep the money you would otherwise be paying to your utilities (power, phone, water etc.) and credit providers. Winning!

Another reason for paying on time is to avoid damaging your credit rating. A credit provider can report late payments and missed payments to a central credit reporting agency. Each late or missed payment can have a negative impact on your future ability to borrow or gain credit.

Imagine you decided not to pay your phone bill, and your phone provider reported the missed payment. That pesky 'missed' payment could negatively impact your future ability to borrow money. How bad could you feel if the 'missed' bill stopped you from buying a family home? Implications of missing and late payments can be more far-reaching than you could ever imagine. And we'll look at that more in *Chapter 7 Loans and Leverage*.

A budget is a financial tool to help you:

* manage your spending
* reach your financial goals
* get out of debt
* ensure you have extra money available for the unexpected
* reduce your stress levels because you know where you stand financially.

As you work on a budget, first look at expenses and then your total income for the same period of time. A budget needs to cover the big picture—a whole year of expenses—because not all expenses happen weekly or monthly. Your big picture budget should capture all of your costs and look at the overall picture of your income and expenditure.

It doesn't matter what date your 'big picture budget' year starts, but it *is* really important to make sure you calculate costs over a full year. That way you catch all of your costs, even the ones you would prefer to forget about. If you don't capture all of your costs you *will* be in for a nasty shock at some stage through the year. You are guaranteed to end up with more bills than money and that doesn't work!

Once you've sorted the big picture number, you can then set up mini-budgets within the big picture budget. It helps manage cash flow more easily and really helps manage lots of ongoing regular costs—those bills you pay monthly or fortnightly. When bills go up, remember you need to tweak the amount of money allocated to that section of your budget, otherwise there will come a time when there's not enough money to meet your planned expenses. Plus, if you add to expenses you *have* to cut the equivalent amount from other costs.

Once you've worked out your total expenses, the next step is to subtract the amount of your total costs from your total income to see whether you have a surplus (+) or shortfall (-).

Expenses can be divided into categories such as:

* essential living (e.g. food, personal care, child care, education, hairdressing)
* lifestyle (e.g. alcohol/cigarettes, postage, music, recreation, dining out, sport)
* home and utility (e.g. rent, mortgage, electricity, gas, water, body corporate fees, phone, internet)
* transport (e.g. registration, insurance, public transport, fuel, servicing, tyres)
* external advice and professional services (e.g. accountant, doctors, dentist, pharmacy, alternative therapists, veterinarian)
* insurance (e.g. home, home contents, motor vehicle, health fund, life covers, ambulance, income protection)
* banking (e.g. account/loan fees, credit card fees, banking package fees)
* household upkeep (e.g. repairs, renovations, maintenance, furnishings, carpet cleaning, painting)
* investment property related (e.g. insurance, rates, body corporate, maintenance, interest)
* memberships/subscriptions (e.g. credit cards, pet grooming)
* miscellaneous.

Examples of income could be:

* salary/wages
* bank interest
* business income
* family tax payment
* pensions
* retirement income stream payments.

At the back of this book, in the Appendix, is a budget template listing lots of possible expenses and income. You can use that budget sheet for *Mind Your Money Activity 1*, where you will create your budget and see where your finances are at.

If you often find you don't have enough money to pay your bills or save, your budget is going to show you where your money is going. It's time to take the blinkers off. Whatever the end balance ends up being in your budget, it is the beginning of your journey to financial freedom and abundance. If you have a history of mismanaging money and not reaching your financial goals and dreams, this is a new start.

Before you start stressing, take a deep breath and relax. I'm sure I heard some of you mutter, 'Relax? You crazy woman ... I can't even begin to think about relaxing when I'm thinking about this sort of thing!' If you're really feeling this way, I suggest you skip this 'job' *temporarily*; you can do it after you finish the book, or at a time when you're feeling less stressed. Promise me you'll come back to it. It *is* the key to your long-term success.

Regardless of your frustration, it is so important you read the rest of the book. There's so much more to learn, so please be kind to yourself. This is only the first of many hurdles you could face as you progress through this journey.

Emotions and money

If you're finding emotions rising up at this point, it's good to understand that another hurdle could be your emotions and finances are intrinsically linked and you haven't been aware of it. It's extremely common for emotions and money to be closely interwoven, especially if there's been a history of abuse and emotional manipulation or control relating to money.

Women are frequently negatively impacted, financially and emotionally, as a result of coming out of a long-term relationship. These impacts are even more pronounced and far-reaching if women leave a domestic violence or abuse situation, particularly where money was a weapon in the relationship and used as a form of control over them and their children. If this was your experience, you might be feeling negative emotions about money. If so, that's okay for the moment.

If lack of money blocked your escape route from the abuse relationship, it's now a tool of freedom, and it's up to you how successfully you will be able to release your negative emotions as you move forwards. It's super important to your future success to release any, and all, negatives you might currently be holding about money. Money needs to be considered as a friend; it is no longer your enemy or a tool of control.

As those nasty emotions come up, I want you to acknowledge the emotions as they rise. Connect to the impact; feel the feelings, wallow in how bad it makes you feel. Can you feel it?

Right about now you're probably thinking, *this woman is stark raving mad*! Some might agree with you, but the reality is I want you to connect to how shitty you feel when overcome by these emotions. Where do you feel it in your body? Does your skin crawl? Do you want to cry? Are you angry? Is your blood boiling? Good. Now that you're feeling its impact, let it go. Otherwise the destruction and corrosiveness of those emotions will warp or destroy your future.

That emotion was a part of your past. It *is* super important to realise its destructive force no longer has to be part of your future. Otherwise you future will be the same old same old.

The choice and power not to allow those emotions to rule your life is *all* yours. Is that what you want? Are you ready to take control? Great, let's do it!

Oh, I almost forgot. Now you've decided those old destructive forces are not going to rule your life, *if and when* they raise their nasty heads I want you to breathe through the emotions and recognise them for what they are—transient feelings designed to take you off track, and more importantly, *know* they will pass.

For centuries women have managed to survive their fears and thrived in spite of their circumstances. You can too! It might sound trite; however, rest assured there is light at the end of the tunnel even if you can't see it right now.

Tracking progress

When you're on a weight loss program, your weight loss coach, even if it's you, tracks your success on a chart or tool. I want you to begin thinking of your budget as a tool to show you how you are improving, that your cash flow is better. I want you to notice your new financial mindset is beginning to create a financial future, one less fraught with potential for emotional mine fields and ticking time bombs. It's time to start being proud of how far you've come and to begin implementing some new strategies. As you learn the tips and tricks in this book, you can almost guarantee you will end up adjusting those initial budget figures. You might even do it more than once as you start proactively working towards your goals.

If you're ready to take on your numbers now, read the instructions below and skip to the Appendix at the end of the book. You can also download the PDF templates of the budget on my website here: **www.womenmindyourmoney.com.au.** There is also an interactive version where you can directly enter your figures and it does the calculating for you, which is available as a bonus for all my readers.

Create A Budget *Mind Your Money Activity 1*

Grab a calculator, your payslips, receipts/invoices, and bank and credit card statements. It's time to get down and dirty with your finances to work out where your money goes.

Do this exercise in pencil in case you want or need to revisit this section time and time again. It will also make it much easier to adjust your numbers, particularly if there is a shortfall of income when compared to your expenditure.

Start filling in figures in the budget sheet at the Appendix in the back of the book. You can also use the Prosperity Budgeting spreadsheet mentioned above.

As you fill in 'expense items', 'income items' and 'budget surplus/shortfall calculation' tables, be realistic. This is not the time to fluff around; it's time to be brutally honest with yourself about how and where you spend your money as you need to know your real starting point. First, list all expenses.

1. In the first column (frequency) record how often you need to pay that particular expense. Is it a one-off, weekly, fortnightly, monthly, quarterly or annual cost? This determines how often the expense has to be paid and tells how many times to multiply the expense to work out the annual cost e.g. weekly x 52; fortnightly x 26; monthly x 12; annually x 1.
2. The second column (frequency amount) is where you record the amount you pay each time you pay the expense.
3. To get the answer for the third column (annualised expense), multiply the expense by the frequency amount. For example: $100 per week x 52 = $5200 per annum.
4. Add up all your expenses listed in the annualised expense column.
5. Next, calculate total income after tax, following the same process you used for expenses—amount per pay multiplied by the number of pay periods in a year. Add up all income listed in the Annualised Income column. Be sure to use your after-tax income after tax amount in your calculations, otherwise you'll end up with numbers that don't tell the true picture of your financial situation.
6. Subtract total expenses from your total after-tax income and you'll be able to see if you have a surplus or shortfall.

If you get a negative figure in the *total surplus/shortfall* section in the table the first time you do this exercise, you've got a shortfall in your income when compared to your expenditure. In other words, you're overspending. It's not the end of the world; it's your new starting point for more adjustments. The bottom line is you have to correct a shortfall; your numbers need to at least break even. Breaking even means just that—the amount you spend must equal what you earn (after tax). If you have a surplus of income over expenses, that's a winning combination.

After taking the time to 'do' your budget, you are probably now aware of where you could be overspending and where there is potential to begin cutting back. Why not grab an eraser and begin trimming your spending right now? Once you've done a bit of trimming on paper, you will need to start matching your actual spending with your proposed spending. Only then will you begin to gain back control.

You may look at that newly created budget and think, *I've tried this before. It doesn't work. I'll start out with good intentions and fail.* If you have a history of mismanaging money or not reaching your financial goals and dreams, you may well have to actually take a step back. Start by looking at your relationship with money and your mindset before you abandon your budgeting efforts. Yes, your mindset will need to be addressed so you can avoid adding to any previous mistakes. Don't worry; we're going to deal with that soon in *Chapter 1 Money Relationships* and *Chapter 2 Money Mindset Makeover*. And then you can look at adapting your money habits in *Chapter 3 Take Control*.

For now, let's look at practical budgeting methods you can put in place straight away.

Budgeting Methods

Now you know what your expenditure is, how are you going to budget to make sure you have the money when you need it for specific bills? There are lots of ways to manage your budget, yet there is no one correct way. Managing a budget is not a one-size-fits-all strategy; what works for your friend probably won't work for you. However, it is important to find the right way for *you* to manage your budget.

Your budget is all about personal preference and making sure the method you choose works for you. It's hard to believe in this era of technology, but one of my friends found an old-fashioned way worked best for her—The Envelope Method.

The Envelope Method

For many years now, my friend has consistently used a bundle of labelled envelopes to manage the family finances. Picture a stack of envelopes labelled electricity, food, fuel, music lessons, sport, holidays and so on. This is the method she uses and her budget works. She's tried other ways, but using envelopes was the only way she could get her head around making her budget work for her family.

To figure out how much she needed for each envelope over a year, she sat down with her previous year's bills, her bank statements and even considered proposed costs, ones that hadn't been included in the previous year's spending. (These were *new* costs relating to her children's private schooling and after-school activities). Once she had figured out how much she needed for each envelope each year, she divided that amount by the number of pay periods. For her, this meant the annual amount was divided by 26 as both she and her husband were paid fortnightly.

One example was her daughters' music lessons, which cost $90 per week just for lessons. There was also the cost of music books and competitions, which equated to at least another $22 per week. She decided she would round the total required up to $115 per week then multiply the amount by 52, meaning she was committed to putting $5,980 aside each year to cover the cost of her daughters' music lessons. She knew the girls had lessons for 48 weeks of the year, so she figured the extra money she saved each week would cover any unexpected costs related to the girls' passion for music. Based on the annual amount she figured out she needed to allocate $230 each fortnight to her envelope.

She is incredibly strict; applying the process above to each of her envelopes (effectively each envelope represents a 'group' of costs), ensuring a pre-determined amount of money is placed into each envelope each pay day. According to her process, the only way money comes out of an envelope is to pay the appropriate bill.

The way I see it, the biggest risk in using this method is someone finding your stash of envelopes and making off with your money. Otherwise, if it works, it works.

The Separate Bank Account Method

With internet banking, if you don't have a home loan, the simplest and safest method is to set up a fee free bank account in which to deposit your savings for bills. Having a prescribed bank account designed to hold money to meet your regular bills is a great idea. Effectively, the account becomes a tool to allow you to manage your regular obligations.

To ensure the process works, you need to allocate enough money each pay period to the account to cover your expenses. To know how much to allocate, you will initially need to work out your annual costs then add about 10% to the calculated total; this extra 10% is to account for inflation and ever-increasing costs. After you've calculated an annual amount, divide it by the number of pay periods in a year; this will give you the amount you need to allocate to your bills account each pay period.

Formula to calculate how much to save each pay period:
(sum of all annual costs + 10%) ÷ no. of pay periods per year

By making a commitment to putting money into an account you are creating a structure that will ensure you can pay your bills as they become due.

A little warning … In the initial stages of setting up this process, there is a chance you could hit a few snags if you have a lot of large bills due all at once. While I acknowledge it will be frustrating, don't give up; setting the process up will remove a lot of financial discomfort in the future. One of my sons uses this method and it works well for him.

The Offset Account Method

If you have a mortgage, there could be an even better way for you to manage your budget than the separate bank account method. In many cases it's possible that your mortgage provider might also provide an option to add an offset account to your loan. If it's possible to add an offset account to your mortgage, it's a super-efficient way to start saving interest charges on your outstanding loan amount.

Let's look at what an offset account can do. Depending on the style of loan you have, it might be possible for any balance you accumulate in an offset account to save you paying interest charges on that very same amount.

Say you have $5000 in savings. If you transfer that amount to a 100% offset account linked to your mortgage, you won't earn interest on the balance; however, you will save the interest charges on that amount now sitting in an offset account.

As borrowers, we always pay a higher interest rate for borrowings than we can hope to earn on the amounts we lend the bank, meaning the money we put into a savings or transaction account. As a result there should be a clear financial advantage to you in using an offset account when compared to letting your money sit in either a transaction account or a high interest savings account. The table below illustrates it fairly simply:

Amount in Account	Annual Interest Earned on Transaction Account###	Annual Interest Earned on Savings Account*	Annual Interest Saved Mortgage^	Maximum Overall Benefit
$5000.00	$0.50	$200.00	$261.50	$261.00

Earnings rate 0.01% pa (transaction account)
*Earnings rate 4.00% pa (high interest account)
^ Comparison rate 5.23% pa

An offset account works very much the same way as having a prescribed bank account when it comes to managing your budget. The offset account holds the money to meet your regular bills; it also can hold your savings and has potential to build up in value over time. The offset account is a tool that allows you to manage regular obligations *and* save you interest on part of your loan balance at the same time. The more money you have in an offset account, the less interest you end up paying on your outstanding loan balance. Winning!

* * *

Remember, there is no perfect way to manage your budget; it's all about personal preference. What is important is to manage your budget rather than letting your money manage you. Yet for any of the strategies we've talked about to work in the long term, we've got to look at what's going on inside that mind of yours. If we don't do that, your current beliefs and mindset may very well sabotage your attempts at putting these strategies to work.

If your budget is in the red, it's a sure sign that your relationship with money needs an overhaul through a *mindset makeover*. So get ready for the next step in shaping your new financial future—looking at your current relationship with, and beliefs about, money. This is *so* important because chances are other people's experiences and ill-advice is driving *your* financial decisions. Having ill-fitting beliefs can come with a huge price and you're the only one who ends up paying!

If nothing changes in your perception and thinking, you are guaranteed to continue to fail. And we don't want that! Are you ready to shape your new mindset and future? Then read on.

Mind Your Money Tip

Creating and using a budget is a giant step towards achieving financial freedom. Your future success is worth the effort!

Part 1

GET YOUR HEAD IN THE GAME

Chapter 1

Money Relationships

'Once your mindset changes, everything on the outside will change along with it.'

—Steve Maraboli

If I asked you what your biggest goal was, knowing that you've picked up this book on finances, I'm certain it would have something to do with never having to worry about money. Isn't being financially secure most people's secret desire? It's no secret that it's my goal too! Thanks to a bit of hard work, a great mindset and a sprinkling of opportunity I'm well on my way. Possibly your ideal money situation could be to be paid to be on a never-ending holiday. If you've been supposedly working on those goals for a while, but the goal posts just keep slipping further and further way, I have news for you: *Most likely you are not going to achieve those goals while you have your current money mindset and relationship with money.*

To be successful you will need to make sweeping changes to how you see money and finances. You'll also make changes as to what you think and believe about yourself, your goals and life. I know overcoming my personal fears, as well as overcoming my parents' impact on my money mindset were key factors in allowing me to transform my financial future all those years ago.

If we keep doing the same thing we've always done, we're going to end up with the same results. I did! To add insult to injury, if we don't like the results we're getting, it's quite possible we may passionately hate what's happening to us financially. I did!

It's time to assess your relationship with money, which, regardless of your awareness of it, is directly based on your perceptions, thoughts and beliefs around money. Some might call this 'mindset', others your 'mental framework'. Others might refer to it as their 'operating system'.

In the introduction, I touched briefly on the importance of having the correct operating system. Let me explain a little bit more about what I mean. If you're working with an operating system that doesn't serve you, as I was as a young woman, there's a strong chance you are not getting the results you want. Or worse yet, you could be getting someone else's results, like I did, by working with other people's belief systems.

If you are not getting the results you know you want and deserve, it's time to realise you need to work with an operating system that works *effectively* for you. Hence, the need for a mindset overhaul.

Mindset and beliefs

I imagine you never thought you'd find anything on mindset in a finance-focused book, and to some it could sound like a bit of mumbo-jumbo. Nevertheless, it's time to realise your perceptions, thoughts and beliefs work together with your unconscious mind to create your reality and the results you keep getting.

So that we're on the same page with this discussion, let's look at a few key terms.

Perceptions

Perceptions are how you see the world through personal filters; no two people *ever* have the same perceptions or understanding of a specific situation. Personal perceptions are created from a blend of experiences and include things like past events and experiences, the experience of our parents and what we see with our own eyes. Perceptions can be impacted by religion, education, age and gender. It's important to be aware that your perception of money and how you use it is going to be critical to your future success.

This is where it begins to get a little tricky—where perception and values start to blend. In fact, perceptions, beliefs and values are all interrelated and create the filters through which you view life. Your thoughts, beliefs and values are the hidden parts of you that cause you to continue taking those particular actions that create your reality.

Thoughts, beliefs and values are again *very* personal. No two people have the same thoughts, beliefs and values. They might have the same view on a subject, or be of the same religion; however, they are very different people with very different ways of seeing the same events. We all have our own filters as to how we see life. The funny thing is, many of us have yet to realise that we have inherited some of our filters and belief systems from the key people who impact our lives.

Back to your perception of *money*…

If you decide not to hold some perceived value around the concept of money and what it does for you, you will never have money. Money will run through your fingers faster than you can make it. On the other hand, if you value money too highly, the extreme pursuit of money may very well end up destroying your relationships with people. Having a good relationship with money is important. Some things are more important than others, so it's rather common for it to be a juggling act as you realise the value of money for you; only then will you be able to achieve the ideal balance in your relationship with money. Hopefully, you will achieve that balance as you continue through this book and life.

Individual experiences have impacted our understanding of communal beliefs to create a personal belief system. More importantly, do you realise you are likely to be working with a belief system that is not *just* your own? Your belief system is bound to have a little of your parents' and grandparents' beliefs blended together to create what, until now, you've misguidedly considered to be your own belief system. The results you keep getting might not be what you intended or even hoped for yourself; they could belong to others. Can you identify which results you're having as a result of operating with a belief system that isn't entirely yours? I didn't like the results I got when I was using my parents' belief systems.

Using other people's beliefs and values is a little like putting on half a dozen pairs of glasses at the same time, jumping behind the steering wheel and expecting to see clearly enough to arrive safely at your ideal destination. It's simply not going to work *effectively*.

Unconscious mind

Your unconscious mind makes lots of decisions for you without you being aware of what's going on. Little things like when and how you breathe are decided by your unconscious mind; it even controls the way you drive. How much conscious thought went into your most recent journey behind the steering wheel? Were you aware of taking your foot off the accelerator, placing it on the brake, pressing the clutch in and changing gears, or did you do it unconsciously? If you drive an auto, did you even have to look when you were putting your car in gear?

The last time I consciously thought about driving was with a left-hand drive vehicle and I had to drive on the other side of the road to what I was used to. Blinkers were on the other side of the column and gears needed to be changed with my right hand. It took a bit of getting used to. Traffic was coming from the opposite direction to which I was used to. My super nervous passenger had a few issues too; they kept trying to leap from the passenger seat to get away from the oncoming traffic! As you can imagine, all those things made me very conscious while driving; yet when I jump behind the wheel in Australia I drive without even thinking about the actions required. My unconscious mind is at work.

Now back to perceptions, thoughts, beliefs, values and your unconscious mind. They work together to impact every aspect of your life. But, for the purpose of this book we're only going to look at how they work together to create your money mindset and the impact they have on your relationship with money. Therefore, I hope you can begin to see why I keep saying, '*It's important that your money mindset and relationship with money work for you*'. Only then will you get positive and effective outcomes for yourself. In fact, having the right money mindset and money relationship is absolutely vital to your future success.

Here's how it works in a nutshell.

Your money mindset is the operating system you use for all things money related. It includes your unconscious collection of perceptions, beliefs, values and thoughts that drive your actions (both habitual and non-habitual) in relationship to money. They are all interrelated and are responsible for the results you are getting.

Effectively, your perception of money impacts your beliefs and values around money—collectively called your 'money' or 'financial mindset'. Your thoughts are based on your beliefs and values. Your thinking drives your financial choices, decisions and actions, including spending and savings habits. And your actions create the real-life outcomes you're getting. Is it starting to make sense?

Your money or financial mindset directly impacts your relationship with money and how you deal with it.

Working on your mindset has the potential to pay huge dividends when you get it right.

Whose beliefs?

Do you know where your current money beliefs originated? Are you working with your own beliefs or did you inherit your money mindset from your parents, or maybe somebody else? I unconsciously inherited my original money mindset from my parents, who had probably learned theirs from their parents.

When I relied on those original beliefs it cost me a lot in terms of both money and missed opportunity, way more than I bargained for. Thankfully, after that initial extremely costly mistake, I realised it was possible to change my money mindset and promptly set about changing my way of thinking to one that was going to serve me rather than hinder me. One of my main goals is to help you adopt a positive money mindset, sooner rather than later. It's important to be ready to grasp opportunities as they arise rather than missing out.

Most of us simply weren't taught about money and financial responsibility when we were in school. Our parents were often too busy being parents and providing for us to worry about teaching us about how to manage our finances. When you think about it, were they truly in a position to teach us *positive* money management skills? Too often they were struggling to manage their own finances, let alone be able to teach someone else about how to handle money. We typically have entered the adult world totally unprepared to manage our finances, so it's little wonder people manage to create a mess of their finances when they first start to earn an income and inevitably get into debt.

Most people think they have a great relationship with money. As long as it keeps coming in so they can spend it, they think all will be fine; there's always another pay day next week. For these people money is a tool for instant gratification.

Types of money relationships

Have you ever stopped to think about how you personally view money? Most people don't and stumble from pay period to pay period, blindly hoping they'll have enough to pay the bills.

Most fall into two categories of money relationships or mindsets:

* Money is a *problem* because there's never enough to go round.
* Money is an *effective tool* that provides an access point to opportunities.

People often find *money is a problem* if:

* their actions are controlled or impacted by not having enough money

* they feel they will never get ahead because of having too many bills to pay
* creditors are chasing for payment of what is owed
* bills are way overdue
* they are paying late fees over and over again
* they have the urge to keep spending yet they don't know how it will be possible to pay for what they already owe
* they feel stressed by not having enough money
* they spend more than they earn
* they never have enough money, no matter how hard they work.

Can you relate to any of the above? If so, money is problematic and *is* disempowering you. We will need to do some work on your mindset and personal relationship with money. It's time to win back your power by viewing and using money effectively as a tool that works for you.

According to the dictionary, doing something *effectively* means 'in such a manner as to achieve a desired result'.[2] In the preface, I shared the story of my million dollar mistake. If I'd been smart and used money effectively instead of being afraid of the opportunity, we would have been $1 million richer some 25 years ago. Plus, if we'd been able to harness that missing million, we would be so much better prepared for our eventual retirement—talk about ineffective use of opportunity!

Let's look at some examples of using money effectively. Consider the two following opportunities. I have $10 000 available to spend on either of these options; the aim is to be able to make a profit at the end by re-selling the asset I buy in 12 months. We are looking for the most *effective* investment:

* I can put money in the bank; it will not go down in value and is guaranteed to pay interest.
* I can start a share portfolio; the share market is down a bit at the moment so there could be some good opportunities around. Australian shares pay income and the value of my investment could go up or down.

---

2 www.oxforddictionaries.com

Putting money in the bank with an investment return of 3% per annum for a year sees me get a total return of $10 300. There are no entry or exit fees.

On the other hand, the share portfolio comes with the potential for dividends (income) to be paid each six months, so I should get two lots of income in a year. Then there's the chance of capital appreciation (increases) should the share market rise. I also don't have any costs associated with holding the shares after my initial brokerage cost of, say, $150. This would allow us to buy shares in five separate companies to diversify our portfolio and reduce the overall level of risk within a share portfolio. If we were to get a 5% income return, and no capital growth, the capital value would be worth $10 350 (after allowing for costs).

We have the potential of a profit with the shares, not a guaranteed value. The way I look at it, the bank investment is an ineffective use of $10 000 when compared to the share portfolio. The share portfolio has the potential to end up being a more *effective use of capital*, particularly if you include a degree of protection by diversifying and investing across a range of companies versus a single company.

You might have noticed the use of 'diversifying' in the paragraph above. The reason for touching on diversification across a range of companies is to introduce the concept as a strategy that can be used to reduce the risk of complete loss of your capital (the money you put into an investment). In simple terms, the benefit of diversification is if one company you've invested in hits hard times (as one friend likes to say, they 'bomb out'), when you have a range of investments rather than a single investment, there is a *much* better potential for you to ride any financial storm than if you had all your investment dollars in a single company. An old adage that explains diversification is the phrase, 'Don't put all your eggs in one basket'.

From a professional and practical point of view, the share portfolio idea has great potential to provide a positive investment outcome, particularly after consideration of holding costs. In my eyes, buying a share portfolio would be an *effective* use of money compared to putting money in the bank.

You may find well-meaning yet unqualified family members, friends and colleagues giving you an opinion as to whether you're doing something 'properly', rather than effectively. Doing something properly means you are operating in a way that is considered right or correct. Yet who determines what is right or correct for you? *You do*, of course. However, you can guarantee your would-be adviser won't know if you are doing 'it', whatever it is, as *effectively* as you could be to benefit you and your particular situation.

As the old saying goes, 'Money makes money'. Firstly, you have to gain back control so you can gather some money together to take advantage of opportunities that will come your way.

Healthy relationships

Contrary to what you may have heard, money is not the root of all evil. It is simply a tool for us to learn to harness.

How you choose to use money is entirely up to you.

Some people love money, others hate it. Some consider money to be an energy exchange; others see it as a value exchange. Money is neither good, nor is it evil; it is simply a tool of exchange.

How you perceive and use money—your money mindset and money relationship—is very personal and is often the result of fear, yours and other people's. Think about how your parents were with money and you may realise where some of your money beliefs come from.

Your relationship with money is often simply a reflection of either how you've used money or money has used you in the past. The good news is your perception of money can change!

I used to operate from a position of fear in relation to money, thanks primarily to parental conditioning and experience. However, as a result of my million dollar lesson, I soon learned to see money as something that could create opportunities, a tool I could harness to create wealth to ensure the security of my family.

As each new 'opportunity' arose, I learned to measure any potential reward available. Let me clarify what I mean by 'opportunity'. It's a chance to consider my willingness to participate in an investment. It doesn't mean I have to do something or commit my money to anything; it's simply a matter of taking the time to measure all aspects of the 'opportunity' and to make a choice that suits me and accommodates my circumstances.

My decision needs to include potential rewards that might be available if I am willing to make a decision—and yes, sometimes take a measured risk—rather than worrying about what might happen if something went wrong and being crippled by fear. On the other side of the reward equation is risk. That aspect needs to be considered too, because it's the part where you have potential to lose your initial investment or have the value of your investment go down. It's important to remember there is no known investment that comes with only rewards; there will be hidden risks somewhere in the equation, so keep digging until you find them.

For me, overall rewards have outweighed the risks involved in the decisions made, so I'd have to say the risks taken have been worth it. I am being totally honest when I say not all outcomes have been to my advantage, which is why it's super important to ensure you diversify your investments and limit the amount you stand to lose if things go pear shaped.

Over the years I've certainly learned not to let a *small* degree of fear stop me; I measure the risks involved before making a decision to take advantage of an 'opportunity'. Many times my mother has been horrified by the measured risks I have taken, simply because they were totally outside of her comfort zone and sometimes well beyond her comprehension. It's not that she's a silly person; she simply couldn't get her head around why anyone would want to do what I did. However, those measured risks she thought were crazy were *well* within the new comfort zone I had developed for myself, and I was the one who reaped the rewards.

The keys to developing a healthy relationship with money are knowledge and a bit of practice. The knowledge contained in this book could be your starting point to developing your own healthy relationship with money. The practice will be up to you.

Beliefs are a powerful ingredient in developing a healthy relationship with money. They drive our decision-making processes and the way we view ourselves and life in general. Let's now look at some positive beliefs that will support a journey to financial abundance.

* Money is an effective tool.
* Money and spirituality do mix.
* The Universe is abundant and you deserve abundance.

Money as a tool

Seeing money as a tool is a fairly alien notion to most people. It used to be to me, but not anymore.

When I think back to that initial investment opportunity being offered, I was essentially being told: 'There is a really great opportunity I'd like us to participate in; it has the potential to make us all very wealthy if only we are willing to take a measured risk'. Based on my filters at the time, I was *not* hearing 'opportunity'; all I heard was the potential for associated risk and loss and feeling a *huge* dose of fear.

If the investment 'opportunity' had been offered in a way that triggered my interest, or maybe even piqued my greed, there is a possibility I may have had a different response than the 'no' I threw at that 'opportunity'. Why? Because the opportunity was originally offered in a manner that directly triggered *all* of my worst fears. It also highlighted my lack of ability to recognise opportunity when it was presented. I had absolutely no idea opportunity often turns up with its mates, risk and reward. At the time all I could think was, *We can't afford to take the risk! What if something goes wrong?* Clearly my fears were screaming for attention. It also tells me I was not seeing money as a potential tool for wealth creation. Oh, can I measure the cost of not being prepared and open to opportunity!

On the other hand, if I had been asked the same question after developing the thought processes of a person who sees money as a tool, the answer would have been entirely different. Now, because I operate totally differently, I begin by asking about the cost of entry to the opportunity and researching the merits of the opportunity before ruling it out or deciding to participate in a viable opportunity with potential for making a profit. No opportunity is ruled out anymore without proper consideration of its merits (reward) and the associated dark side (risk).

Now is a great time to ask things like: 'Have I been seeing money as a tool? Will I be in a position to take advantage of opportunities when they arise?' Sadly, the answer is *probably not.* I find people simply are not prepared unless they start changing their mindset so they are able to see and use money as a tool.

A person who sees money as a tool weighs up each opportunity as it is presented. They decide whether to act upon opportunities or not, rather than being held to ransom by a lack mentality, or worst yet, the impact of a fear mentality.

A person who sees money as a tool weighs up each opportunity as it is presented.

I mentioned in the preface that during the Global Financial Crisis (GFC), some clients were devastated both financially and emotionally by their losses. However, there were some great opportunities about if you had cash or access to credit. It was all about conviction and timing.

Let me explain...

During the GFC my husband was very nervous. He had been listening to media reports, which at the time were predicting financial doom and gloom—catastrophe even! He began talking about selling our share holdings at bargain basement prices, which would have locked in substantial financial losses.

Not only was I hearing this fear from clients, I was hearing it at home too. Argh! I was hearing everything I did not want to hear. My husband was looking to sell and take losses, while I was looking at the potential for future growth in share prices and to buy more. How different could we be? We discussed our positions and clearly his was fear-based—sell before we lose any more was his attitude. I was thinking along the lines of seeing an opportunity to snatch up bargains. What a contrast!

After much toing and froing, without being able to make a joint decision, I eventually thought outside of the box to explain why we should take the opportunity to buy, rather than be paralysed by fear. I compared the situation with bargain shopping at the local, high-end department store; however, the same principal works regardless of where you choose to shop. I put it in terms that made sense to him: Imagine the item you were planning to buy was suddenly reduced to half price because the store was having a 50 per cent off sale. Would you be tempted to take advantage of the discount? Maybe even buy two for the usual price of a single item? Of course you would ... unless you would prefer to pay full price. Not likely!

The decision to invest, or not, is all about timing and opportunity.

When you consider the item you are buying is exactly the same quality, regardless of what you pay, you're going to get the exact same quality merchandise. How much you pay simply depends on timing.

When you go shopping, regardless of whether you are buying basic lifestyle requirements or investments, who really wants to pay full price? I know I don't; I love a bargain!

Let me give you our real life example.

Mid-GFC our superannuation fund had money to invest and we needed to make some investment decisions: to continue to hold cash or to begin buying additional shares. On the table for consideration was: would our super fund spend $10 000 to buy Commonwealth Bank (CBA) shares or continue to sit in cash investments?

Pre-GFC we knew CBA shares were sitting at a price of around $65 per share. Mid-GFC the price had fallen to around $25 per share. Company management was still the same, the company's business growth strategy was still the same and dividends were high. However, instead of paying $65 for one share, we could effectively get two for the price of one and have some cash left over. Effectively, we could buy 400 shares for what we would previously have paid for 153 shares. Bargain!

If the super fund did a bit of 'bargain shopping' and bought some shares, this meant at least two and a half times as much potential for capital appreciation (increased value), coupled with more than two and a half times as much tax-effective income for the same amount spent. As it turned out, when the proposal to buy shares was explained that way, I gained my husband's agreement to begin buying more shares for our superannuation fund at the bargain price of $25 each. They are now sitting at around $90 each. You do the maths. The original $10 000 investment has turned into $36 000 in value, plus the investment keeps paying regular income every six months, which has been used to buy even more shares. In my view this is winning!

The moral of the story is: Money, when used effectively, can allow you to select which of life's opportunities you want to be in a position to take advantage of.

Being spiritual and rich

Contrary to what you've heard, being spiritual and rich do mix. They work together well.

Perhaps some of your current money beliefs have come from a particular spiritual path or even from a past life. Your spiritual belief may promote austerity and advocate giving up wealth or assets. In some circles there's a widely held belief that you can't be spiritual and rich. This is one belief I refuse to accept! Spirit wants us to live an abundant life, not one of suffering. Money is a tool for use for the greater good. A tool to allow people to contribute to the support of others—others less fortunate than Spirit allows us to be. Does that put a new slant on being spiritual and having money at your disposal?

The belief about spirituality and being poor has often been perpetrated by very large and wealthy institutions—think of what some churches tell their followers. Living conditions of some church hierarchy certainly don't support that they've taken vows of poverty! I've been to the Vatican, as well as many other churches and temples around the world, and can tell you those surroundings are absolutely sumptuous in comparison to the surroundings in which the supporters of the organisation live.

Here's something to consider when you are deciding whether it's possible for you to be spiritual and rich. If you were to become wealthy in the future, could you:

* make a difference in another person's life, or possibly many peoples' lives, if you had money
* provide employment for others so they too can provide for their family

* give to charities or the under-privileged
* give away part of your fortune or income to create a foundation for the benefit of others?

I ask myself, how can being spiritual and rich be wrong when you are able to use your wealth for the benefit of others? In my view it can't!

Universal abundance: Are you ready to receive?

I'm frequently called a hippy by both family and friends because of my personal beliefs; in fact, being a hippy is something I'm quite proud of, even if I don't dress like your typical hippy in highly colourful, flowing clothing. To me, being a hippy means I think outside of the box and have beliefs that are not always considered to be mainstream.

For someone with a background in money, not to mention quite a bit of formal education and training, being a hippy probably sounds more than a bit weird. I want to share some of those beliefs because I know the difference being able to blend my hippy side and professional knowledge has made to my life. I fully appreciate the support the Universe provides in a multitude of ways.

Be aware that not all support the Universe provides is monetary; sometimes it can be opportunities that come up on your radar. Often I've had people comment that I've been 'in the right place at the right time' to benefit from an opportunity. Being open to what the Universe is able to provide means recognising and acting on the opportunity when it arises, not being frozen in fear of 'what if?' Worse yet is being so out of tune with yourself that the Universe isn't able to communicate with you because you simply aren't open to communication.

Remember those CBA shares we purchased during the GFC? That was a combination of identified opportunity (that is, reduced pricing identified as a result of my training), conviction (my training) and belief (training and belief in the Universe), as well as being able to convince my husband to act (thanks for the shopping analogy, Universe); all working together to achieve the desired result.

Another time was when I was certain that I had just blown a job interview with a very reputable company that dealt primarily with share investments and high net worth (rich) clients. At the time, I knew very little about shares even though I was hungry for knowledge and willing to learn more. While I was sure I'd never hear from them again, they called the very next day to offer me a position that came with a $10 000 pay increase and a fully paid company car. Thank you Universe; you knew I needed to escape from my cranky old boss (you know, the one who used to yell at me all the time for humming to myself) and you delivered an outcome far better than I could have imagined. I even got a wonderful new boss as part of the bargain.

Would you believe the Universe even helped us find our house? Thanks to an ad in a real estate window we were led to a house on a street that was elevated and might offer views. We had a little bit of a snoop around the neighbourhood, only to discover three other houses for sale in the street. Yes, we were 'lucky' enough to buy one of those properties; 'lucky' too that the bank thought it was a good opportunity and agreed to lend us the money to complete the purchase. Thanks Universe for the opportunity. We also relied upon my training to know how to manage to pull the deal together. I knew we needed finance approval and settlement before I could resign from work to move to Queensland. I even trusted the Universe to find me a new job so I could pay off the loan we'd just got. I'm happy to say the Universe delivered yet again when I needed it, but enough about me. Did you realise the Universe is chock-a-block full of abundance, and there's enough for all of us?

You have to be ready and open to receiving what is energetically and rightfully yours under Universal laws.

Worthiness

Could you possibly be blocking yourself from receiving? Until I realised the power of my thoughts I had no understanding of the potential to repel money and opportunity.

While my mind is now open to receiving, it hasn't always been that way. The 27-year-old me obviously did not feel worthy of such wealth or success. At the time, my operating system was based entirely on fear and lack. There was no concept of gratitude or receiving; my actions were super effective in repelling the bounty of the Universe. With a faulty operating system, lack of gratitude and no sense of worthiness, no wonder I struggled with my old mindset.

After that very expensive lesson, I realised I had inherited my beliefs and values from my parents. Neither had any appreciation of worthiness or gratitude really; all they knew was hard work. To add insult to injury, my mother came complete with a particularly strong fear mentality to boot. There was no way I could possibly be successful or feel worthy with that sort of financial toolkit.

I had no idea about the concept of worthiness way back then. No idea at all. To be where I am spiritually, financially and emotionally, I've worked hard to make-over my inherited belief system and to develop a sense of worthiness. I always used to believe that other people were worthy of, and deserved, success and happiness.

Now I know I deserve and am worthy of personal success and happiness.

At the time of writing, all that personal work, combined with a bit of knowledge and measured risk taking have allowed us to accumulate a range of investments in property, as well as a substantial share portfolio (one hanging out in the seven figure range, dependent on what the share market is doing), cash and even precious metal holdings. Not too bad for a late starter with a serious 'mistake' under their belt, even if I say so myself!

Oh yeah, this is supposed to be about being worthy...

I checked a number of sources on the definition of worthiness. It is a noun that describes 'the state or quality of having value or merit'[3], although this definition really doesn't do it justice.

Feeling worthy is about knowing you really do deserve to receive. To be open to receiving love, good health, happiness and, of course, money and wealth, you have to feel that you deserve to benefit from

---

3 www.en.wiktionary.org/wiki/worthiness

the bounty of the Universe. You have to be willing to take a risk or two along the way, otherwise you will be closing out opportunities to receive; in fact you could be repelling what the Universe is trying to deliver.

I've come to realise having a sense of worthiness, or feeling worthy of something, is directly related to our self-esteem. The way I see it, if my self-esteem is shot to pieces there is absolutely no way I can feel worthy of anything. Forget happiness, love, success, abundance or wealth. There's no space for it my life, simply because I have no connection to it.

On the other hand, if my self-esteem is healthy there's a very strong chance I will feel worthy of everything going right in my life. I will have an expectation of happiness, love, success, abundance and wealth. Because I have a connection to feeling worthy there will be space for worthiness and all the things I could hope for in my life. The Universe will be able to deliver.

Some may laugh; however, I suggest in the short term that you 'fake' feeling worthy if you currently aren't yet up to believing you truly are worthy. I'm sure you've heard the old saying, 'Fake it 'til you make it'. It applies to everything in life except for formal qualifications.

As you start to feel worthy by acting worthy, you'll create new connections in your brain. Connections that accept the concept of you being worthy so you can come to know you are worthy. Remember, feeling worthy is connected to your self-esteem, so it's important to be kind to yourself and not to beat yourself up over it. Go on, give it a try and be nice to yourself. It truly can't hurt.

Without my experiences and array of mistakes (let's be honest I've made more than one error of judgement over the years), I would not have been equipped to help clients get to where they are now. One family of clients in particular have gone from being avid spenders to being conscious of their spending and now appear to be displaying the fruits of feeling and being worthy of financial security. This only happened after we worked together to change their mindset and had a strong 'chat' about what they were missing out on based on their old attitudes.

Before their change of awareness they lived a high life, constantly spending on 'nothing' (their words, not mine) and were always dining out. They now understand their bank and a raft of restaurants were the ones benefiting from the spending and dining habits. Now they're super keen on monitoring their progress on paying down their personal debts. They're no longer 'happy' wasting money; instead they are determined to buy an investment property within 12 to 18 months—something they would never have been able to consider until they changed their mindset. And they are well on their way to achieving their goal.

Recently, I was fortunate to participate in a very interesting discussion on personal worth and value. It's important to know that personal worth is not about money; it's the about the way you feel about yourself. Sometimes we make the mistake of measuring ourselves, and our perceived worth, against others—often those we think are more successful than us. If you're still doing that, it's definitely time to stop; otherwise all you're doing is hurting yourself.

So what is the difference between value and worth? It's a little tricky for some people to differentiate, so let's look at value first. This is a very different concept than the personal values we keep talking about.

One way to think about value is that you get compensated (paid) for the value you bring to your employer, or in the fees you charge for your skills and services when you are self-employed. As an employee I expected to be valued and was financially compensated accordingly. However, when I became self-employed, I admit to struggling with the value I could bring to professional interactions and found myself discounting fees to 'get the gig', so to speak. How could I expect others to value me if I wasn't willing to value myself and my skills?

Your value is related to what other people get out of your interaction, whether it's a professional or personal interaction, or maybe to your relationships.

Let's be clear … In the eyes of Spirit the value of your assets has absolutely nothing to do with your worthiness to be supported. The way Spirit sees it, everyone deserves to be supported and nurtured. Your worth *does* rely on your self-worth. It's important to get that in tiptop condition so you're able to attract what you need in your life. Be careful not to confuse value and worth, they're entirely different things, and it is super important to know the difference.

Be true to yourself, live your worth and know your value.

Self-worth

Self-worth is yet another important component of your personal operating system; it controls *everything* you do. If your operating system is damaged and showing signs of no longer working effectively, nothing is going to go as well as it could. Now is the perfect time to realise your self-worth is directly related to your values and ultimately to how you value and see yourself.

If you are lacking in self-belief you might find yourself struggling with decisions or missing opportunities. If you *do* decide to jump on an opportunity, you could find yourself frozen with fear and end up not taking action. It's possible you've been sabotaging your income potential by not believing in your skills and working for less than you truly are worth. You may have been hampering your career.

It's confronting in today's rather shallow society that we find there is a warped definition of what is valued. External things like outward appearances, assets and the amount you earn seem to be the measure of one's self-worth; unfortunately, this societal focus on the external doesn't help the way we, as individuals, value ourselves. External things have nothing to do with the true worth of a person.

Self-worth has everything to do with how you feel about yourself. The good thing about self-worth is that we aren't stuck with what we've got right now; it can be adjusted and improved with some effort and changing your mindset. A good starting point is to grab a pen and paper, invite a friend for coffee and have them list your good points. All the things they love about you are usually the things you can't see for yourself and therefore aren't able to value.

Grab a pen and paper, invite a friend for coffee and have them list your good points.

Think about the people you know. Can you tell which of your friends truly don't value themselves and those who are truly self-assured? It should be fairly easy to see the differences; the first place to look is how they operate. One will be confident on all levels—physical, mental and emotional. The other is likely to be in a state of emotional chaos, frequently facing decisions they can't make and holding a poor self-image; in fact, they will be far from confident in most, if not all, aspects of life. Another consideration is the quality of decisions they make. Are they making good decisions or are they unable to make decisions (trapped in fear)? Worse yet, are they making downright damaging decisions?

I too have been in that deep, dark place of poor self-esteem and self-image. There was a time, after an attempted rape and assault by a friend's husband, compounded by being judged by people who had an opinion but no knowledge of the facts, I got to a point where I considered self-harm. Not my proudest moment, yet looking back I realise I was making totally unbalanced decisions.

I had gone from being a confident, outgoing professional woman to a person struggling with poor self-esteem and agoraphobia; too afraid to go out of the house by myself and terrified to be alone unless I was behind the locked door at home or locked 'safely' in the car. What a combination!

I was on the road a lot for work at that time, so I had lots of time to dwell in that nasty headspace, all on my own; it was a horrible place. I even picked out a tree to drive my car into, reasoning in my own warped way that if the 'accident' happened during work hours my family would be compensated for my loss. Only now can I truly appreciate how clouded my judgement was, and how much despair I must have been in at the time.

The thought of not seeing my three sons grow to be men was the trigger to make me begin working on myself. Thank you, my sons; you unknowingly saved my life that day.

To add insult to injury, I gained a stupid amount of weight in three very short weeks thanks to the anti-depressants I was gobbling; my confidence plummeted and my self-esteem was destroyed. To put it bluntly I was a blubbering wreck, crying at the drop of a hat, yet still forcing myself to try to function normally. It was a losing battle.

It was much easier to overhaul my thought processes than it was to shift that weight. Many years later a small part of that weighty reminder is still with me; getting rid of it is still a work in progress.

The tipping point for me was the realisation that I could 'choose'. I could elect to be a victim for the remainder of my life, having my actions and decisions controlled by fear, or I could pick myself up, dust myself off and get on with making a life of which I would be proud. I chose to get on with making a life that made me happy.

Sharing the story of my dim, dark head space may shock some people, especially those who think they know me, yet I'm simply sharing to prove that it is possible to change your mindset. You are in charge of how you feel about everything, including your self-esteem.

It's okay to receive

Due to your past experiences and beliefs, you might be thinking you don't 'deserve' anything. *That needs to stop now!* Did you hear my cranky voice? If you didn't, you might want to listen again because it was *booming*!

Before doubting your deservedness any further, it would be remiss of me to omit this all-important concept:

It's your right to receive the support of the Universe. Which means it's absolutely fine for us all to receive, and benefit from, Universal abundance.

In fact, the first part of becoming ready and able to accept abundance is simply being aware of the system.

Another part of your trouble with being 'deserving' likely relates directly to your self-worth. Low self-worth brings with it the view that you are not worthy of receiving anything , and certainly not Universal abundance. This blocks the Universe from doing what it's meant to do … deliver. Part of your job is to be willing to receive.

Love yourself

I want you to stand in front of a mirror and really look into your eyes. I want you to look past the colour of your eyes; I want you to look much deeper. You're looking for the inner you, the one you may not really value or the child within that's in need of a hug and more love than you've been giving her lately.

How does looking into your soul make you feel? However you feel is perfect: there is no judgement. It's a starting point as you learn to love yourself again. The first time I tried it I was super uncomfortable, I didn't make eye contact with my little girl. The next time was a little easier—I spent a fleeting moment with her. After that, each time got a little easier. Now I easily connect to my inner self and treat myself much better than ever before. Without self-love we struggle with our self-worth and keep making decisions that aren't in our best interest.

Knowing my own past struggles, you can imagine how happy I was recently to be told twice on the same day by two separate women, 'You would have been so proud of me'. And after they shared their stories I was indeed super proud; these women had stood up for themselves rather than taking the disempowering treatment being dealt out to them. One commented about a boss who was being unfair. 'There's no way I would've stood up to my boss seven years ago.' Seven years ago is when we met; for her to remember our meeting is a testament in itself. To be reminded of the changes she's been able to make … well, that was another matter altogether. It was a real gift to know my encouragement had truly made a difference to her operating system. The self-worth of these lovely ladies is now super healthy; the biggest bonus is their decisions and actions show just how much they value themselves.

Remember, the 'stuff' of values is unable to be quantified in terms of physical measurements. It's more about the quality of the feelings they evoke in you personally. While values are internal and very personal, they directly impact your day-to-day operating systems in ways you've possibly never even thought about. Please make sure your operating system is working at its best. After all, you deserve to be the best version of you possible, and you can't be that with a faulty operating system, can you?

The Universe/Source

A quick heads-up about how the Universe/Source works. When we ask the Universe to provide something, we're asking the Universal supply chain to deliver. Sometimes this can happen quickly; other times it takes a bit longer. Two things that must remain constant are your willingness to receive and also your gratitude when you receive.

It helps to be aware of what the Universe hears. 'Don't' isn't in its vocabulary, so be aware of keeping your thoughts and requests positive. Instead of saying *'I don't want to be broke'* it would serve you better for the Universe to hear you say *'I'm so grateful for the wealth I currently have access to'.* Otherwise you may not get what you thought you requested.

Source is constantly on the lookout for opportunities to provide for us; however, it simply can't provide if we aren't ready and open to receive.

* * *

Now that you understand the importance of having a healthy relationship with money, where your beliefs and perceptions around money serve you rather than hurt you, it's time to be open to the abundance waiting for you. I think you're ready for a *money mindset makeover.*

Mind Your Money Tip

Be open to receive—the Universe can't deliver if you're unconsciously blocking it! Check in with yourself; are you blocking things just by your attitude?

Chapter 2

Money Mindset Makeover

'Money is usually attracted, not pursued.'

—*Jim Rohn*[4]

It's vitally important to make sure your mindset fits the new 'you' and the life you are working to create. While we readily commit to making over our wardrobes, we never seem to give a thought to making over our minds. Our minds are our biggest asset in life; so why have a mindset that isn't serving you well?

Working on making over something as important and far reaching as your mind has potential to pay huge dividends. Imagine how good life could be when you get it right! A mindset makeover does not have to cost you anything other than your time. Yes, it takes time, application and some practice; yet there doesn't have to be a cost in dollar terms. It's worth making an effort to achieve your desired result—a future full of abundance and opportunity.

---

4 www.brainyquote.com/quotes/quotes/j/jimrohn147505.html

Your unconscious mind

As mentioned in Chapter 1, your money mindset is the operating system you use for all things money related. It includes your unconscious collection of perceptions, beliefs, values and thoughts that drive your actions (both habitual and non-habitual) in relationship to money.

It's vital to understand your unconscious mind is just like the Universe/Source... it has absolutely no concept of what the term 'don't' means. The unconscious mind is simply not able to understand or even hear the 'don't' when you say, 'I don't want to be broke'. Your unconscious mind hears, 'I want to be broke'; it completely skips the all-important 'don't' that *you* are so focused on. Because your unconscious mind misses the 'don't', it's going to keep delivering you the 'broke' it hears you ask for.

Your unconscious mind has no idea of time frames either. According to it, everything you see, feel and know is already reality, *and* it will do everything it can to make what you know and feel to remain your reality. If your mind can picture something negative or something you really do not want in your life, you need to realise that because you can feel and 'know' it, you're already part way to getting more of what you prefer not to have.

Focus on what you want in your life. Give absolutely no energy or thought to what you prefer not to have in your life.

The key concept here is: You get what you focus on.

If you focus on the negative things in your life, that is what will continue to be delivered instead. Focus on what it is you want in your life. Give absolutely no energy or thought to what you prefer not to have in your life.

Let me illustrate …

Do you worry about not having enough money? If you do, does worrying really do anything for you? Does it bring you more money? Or does life actually seem to get that little bit harder? In fact, the more you worry the worse you will end up perceiving your situation to be, even feeling like it is hopeless and wanting to give up.

Worrying won't and can't change anything! What it does is set you up for more of the same—creating the reality you do not want—

simply because your thoughts are operating from a position of fear and wallowing in a belief of lack—creating a lack mentality. Remember, I know how it feels; it's downright uncomfortable and is totally disempowering to boot. If you want more of the same results, change nothing and you are guaranteed to continue to fail. What a nasty lesson!

As simple as it seems, a conscious change of mindset, when combined with altered actions, can make a HUGE difference to how you perceive your situation.

It's incredibly important for you to *keep your perceptions and thoughts entirely positive* because those very same thoughts have the ability to create your reality. Remember, there's an ongoing ripple effect from your thoughts to your reality. Be sure to create a future you *really* want.

I know someone who is frequently faced with the need to 'borrow from Peter to pay Paul', as the old saying goes. They're always worried about not having enough money, so guess what they keep getting? There simply never seems to be enough money to go round; an unexpected cost is a disaster that frequently results in them being in debt to obliging family members. I can't image what it does to one's self-worth to be constantly battling with money.

For every single financial step forwards this person takes, inevitably another 'disaster' strikes, getting in the way of continued forward progress. They are constantly living in fear of not having enough, not to mention struggling with a lack mentality that impacts their daily reality because they keep focusing on what they don't want.

Given that the unconscious mind ignores 'don't', the Universe keeps providing everything they truly aren't hoping to attract. Let me share a few strategies to ensure your unconscious mind knows what you *do* want so you get the results you desire.

Ask for what you want

There's a family 'joke' that's gone on for many years now, about my communication with angels and the Universe. My youngest son was driving me to an important medical appointment and he was worried we would be late due to heavy traffic. I silently asked the Universe to clear a path so we would arrive on time, and I told him not to worry because I'd asked the Universe and angels for assistance. Ten minutes later, he commented on what a great run we were having and how many green lights we'd encountered. No sooner were the words out of his mouth than he said, 'Aah, I forgot you're in the car; you always get green lights'. Needless to say, we arrived on time. Thanks again, Universe!

For years, I've been asking my angels for assistance in getting to places on time and safely, and in finding car parks. Each time they provide, I share my gratitude. Amazingly, they are generous enough to continue to provide as long as I continue to show gratitude and don't take them for granted—thanks Universe.

... be aware enough to ask and to be grateful for what you receive.

The same applies when I am grateful to the Universe for the financial abundance and opportunity it delivers; it continues to deliver in many and varied ways, some of them very surprising. You have to be aware enough to ask and to be grateful for what you receive. While we're on the topic, let's have a quick look at gratitude.

Have gratitude

Have you ever stopped to think what 'gratitude' means? According to the Oxford Dictionary[5], gratitude means: 'the quality of being thankful; readiness to show appreciation for and to return kindness'.

To me gratitude is a state of being; sometimes it's even a feeling that permeates my body. It's where I appreciate what I have, who I'm

5 www.en.wikipedia.org/wiki/Lotteries_in_Australia

with or what I have been gifted, and sometimes all three at the same time.

Gratitude has a dual purpose. It serves to recognise the goodness that's evident both within, and outside, ourselves, and also about paying those gifts and habits forward. As you pay 'it' forward, it seems you attract more blessings and benefits.

Gratitude isn't just about items; it's also about experiences. Maybe you've heard someone complaining that they aren't satisfied, wanting something more from life. This is ingratitude at work and is a choice the person makes.

On the other hand, think what happens when you assist someone and they really appreciate your help. Because you feel your actions are valued, you are much more likely to assist the same person, or another, in the future. Now let's apply that concept to Universal abundance.

Think about the possibilities that could open up—how much more the Universe might gift you—if you were grateful for the things you received.

Picture it

So I could enjoy the adventure of my first ever skydive, I created a mental image. I imagined the feeling of exhilaration I would experience; I was excited by the prospect of allowing myself to fall through the sky with the wind in my ears—in short I was super excited to be jumping! The actual experience was *much* better in reality; I buzzed with adrenalin and the intensity of the feeling lasted for days. It was so pleasurable I immediately wanted to do it again. I've managed it three more times so far. I can picture it and can feel the buzz so vividly that I'm ready to go again any time the opportunity arises.

Create a picture of the future as you want it to be.

In contrast, I know people who have pictured everything going wrong, been suited up and ended up unable to exit the plane. Those people got exactly what they pictured—fear, and not being able to achieve their goal. They paid the same amount for the experience; however, they got vastly different results than I achieved.

Create a picture of what you want using mind movies, vision boards or even by writing a list.

A lot of people find things like vision boards bring great results. The visual prompts encourage your subconscious to focus on what you want to achieve.

Feel it

I want you to add in another vital step—start imagining how success *feels.* This is another way to communicate to your subconscious the results you want by telling a story of how the new success feels and sounds.

Feelings and emotions are close friends; they are often the measure we use in making a decision because they have physical impacts on our bodies. Think about how many times you've faced a tough decision and your body felt 'yuck' or 'off in the tummy'—this is your body's way of letting you feel its opinion. With some luck you also will have experienced the physical impacts of emotions like joy and love; they give entirely different feelings in the body. Now I want you to *feel the difference* between the two scenarios outlined below.

Scenario One: You are constantly battling with not having enough money and you concentrate on and lament the fact that you are *always* broke, with next to nothing in the bank, and you owe people money. You know you will have to move yet again and you can't stop thinking about that. It's not just the hassle of moving; you simply can't afford to move. And now, your worst nightmare is coming true because your lease isn't being renewed; you *have* to move. How does this make you feel? Fearful? Insecure? Anxious? Depressed? Hopeless?

Scenario Two: You are concentrating on the money in your bank account—the exact amount does not matter, yet you feel secure. You no longer have to borrow money from accommodating friends and family, and can actually pay some debts back. You are also seeing yourself in a beautiful home that is yours for as long as you choose to live there. You are no longer faced with the prospect of moving. How does all this make you feel? You're probably rejoicing at the feeling of emotional freedom. You feel secure. You may even be breathing freely.

Now you know the feelings of success and security; it's liberating not to be operating from a place of fear. What if you could transfer that feeling of security and knowing you are safe to reality? You can! Remember we talked earlier of concentrating on what you want to achieve, not the things you prefer not to have in your life? That's a first step.

By telling your unconscious mind exactly what you want and how it feels, you are much closer to transferring the feelings and results into reality.

Open your eyes to opportunity

Be aware of what Source, or the Universe, is offering. Start by noticing recurring ideas, events, reminders, opportunities or even introductions. Some people refer to recurring events as synchronicity. Macquarie Dictionary views synchronicity as 'the occurrence of two unrelated events at the same time, which appears to have some significance but which in fact has none'.[6]

Synchronicity can include recurring songs on the radio or signs you see in the environment surrounding you. These recurring or synchronous events could be the way the Universe is trying to deliver opportunities to help with what you need, or to even showcase those talents you keep hiding.

I kept being led towards writing a book; the idea came up at least three times, from three very different sources, before I was really

6 www.macquariedictionary.com.au/features/word/search/?word=Synchronicity&search_word_type=Dictionary

listening and in a position to run with it. First, I'd been told it would help to build credibility in my field if I had a publication of some sort available on my website. The second was after a discussion about a financial debacle a friend was suffering, when she said, 'You should write a book; you know so much'. Finally, I went to a networking event focused on being a key influence in your field and the key tool was to write a book on your field of expertise. All those external drivers coupled with the fact that I appear to have a love of words finally got through.

With my personal insecurities finally overcome, Source had a chance to provide what I had been attempting to ignore. For quite a while I had wallowed in fears and discounted my knowledge, experience and skills. Opportunity eventually knocked so insistently that I couldn't ignore it. I have put myself, my knowledge and beliefs on the line, so that hopefully I can make a difference to the lives of others by equipping them with their own knowledge and skills. Hence, this book and workshops plus public speaking; it's surprising what's happening now that I've allowed myself to get over my fears.

If you've told the Universe clearly what you want to do or receive, it may come in unexpected ways. For many years I looked at ways to empower people, including myself, and told the Universe that I would like to work in my passion; that is, to work with women to empower them to overcome poor self-belief and mindset. Would you believe I completed a personal development course, which I thought was just to help me in my own growth, and came away with qualifications and skills around empowering people's mindset? Before participating, I had absolutely no idea there would be a qualification as an outcome of the course. Talk about the Universe being efficient.

This is another example of the many ways the Universe provides. Keep your eyes and ears open for what's coming to you too.

It's absolutely imperative to be clear and positive about what you are seeking to achieve.

Tell your unconscious mind truly what you want now; otherwise you might end up getting something you really do not want!

Set an intention

As humans we think the world runs to a timetable. We're ever so conscious of this when we use planes, trains or buses; especially if we're running late. Yet it's important for us to realise, while we might set a time by which a goal or outcome is to be achieved, we may need to be a little bit flexible where the Universe's timing is concerned. After all, Universal Law is a law unto itself!

I mentioned earlier that I put my faith in the Universe to find a job when we moved to Queensland. I decided a month off work would be fine, reasoning everybody would be settled at school and university, the house would be sorted out and everything unpacked.

The Universe had other ideas. Regardless of how many interviews I had, I was unsuccessful or the employer wanted to pay me about half of what I was used to earning. It took three months for the right opportunity to appear. I was mentally bored and beginning to worry about my employability; only then did the Universe decide to deliver. While I was waiting impatiently, the kitchen was renovated and other major works completed. Obviously the Universe decided I needed more time and rest than I'd anticipated and wanted those renovations done and dusted before it was ready to provide a job.

A little tip ...

If you want to speed things up, stop thinking of the future—think now.

The thing to remember is your unconscious mind works on the here and now. You need to think *now* how you will feel when the goal is achieved. You need to be feeling it *now* if you want to get your unconscious mind on board to help you with your goal being achieved.

I know one very successful person, a personal mentor, who uses this method successfully. She takes a mental snapshot of how things will look once she's achieved her goal. The next step is to combine it with how she will feel knowing she's been successful in achieving her goal. She goes into detail, determining what the surroundings will look like and the sounds she will hear; for example, she will be looking out from the stage to a group of women who are avidly listening to her speak and applauding her at the end of her presentation. She's that specific. She brings all of the images, feelings and knowing related to her success together and allows her unconscious mind to work its magic. She's realistic; she knows the Universe needs some time to deliver. She's doing what she loves and is passionate about. Recently, she shared that she is about three years ahead of where she thought she would be on her personal timeline regarding the results she's been achieving. Her final comment was, 'Thank you, Universe'.

What I Want *Mind Your Money Activity 2*

How many years of accumulated negativity are stored in your head? It really doesn't matter because you are going to break free of the negative mindset with which you've been operating. You need to be clear on what you want in your life. This exercise is where the rubber meets the road, where you picture what you want your life to look like and start the process of creating it. Imagine how liberating it will be to have a more abundant life, one free from financial worries.

Grab some paper because you're about to create a list, focusing on what you want your life to look like; in other words, the things you want your life to provide you. It can be anything from financial ease and flow, to having an overseas holiday to your ideal annual destination—even a description of your ideal life partner. It's your list, so be sure to be very clear on what it is you want in your life.

What I Want My life to look like—Things I Want in My Life
e.g. financial ease and flow

To give you a few ideas, not in any particular order, my list includes things like: health and vitality; financial ease and flow; family; love; annual overseas travel for four weeks to a place that interests me (nobody else); regular speaking engagements; success with the on-line coaching program and workshop formats I'm busy creating. If you want to be more specific on the money front, be aware that could cap your future earnings capacity. Let's say you decide you'd like to earn $50 000 each year and you're currently earning $35 000; what if a job comes along that suits you to a tee yet it pays $80 000? Because the Universe can only deliver what you ask for, it would not even present the opportunity to you. When it comes to money, it pays not to be too specific as you might limit your success.

Now take a really good look at your list of *what you want your life to look like*. It's time to move forward, using your list as a guide, to create the future you want for yourself.

I recommend keeping your list where you can see it. It will act as a powerful reminder of exactly what it is you want the Universe to help you create in your life. You should see the list of reminders to both me and the Universe on my office wall; we are on track!

If you're really visual, create a vision board for your future.

If you were to enter my office, you may find vision boards, goal lists or even a paraphrased reminder that 'Impossible is not a fact; it's an opinion', from the great Muhammad Ali.[7]

Vision boards are a reminder to the Universe and I of what 'we' are focused on. I'm grateful for what's been delivered and what's on its way. It's common for me to update or create a new board; timing depends on the results already achieved.

Or, if you prefer, you could create a mental image so you can see, feel and know your end game. You can take your image with you everywhere. Be sure to make it a powerful and clear image of the future you want.

The flip side of the 'what you want' list is *to be clear about what you are ready to release to the Universe*—things that are no longer serving you or are holding you back from being the best you can be.

Once you and the Universe have achieved some of your visions, consider creating some more visualised goals so the Universe has an opportunity to continue to provide.

---

7 www.goodreads.com/quotes/121663-impossible-is-just-a-big-word-thrown-around-by-small

What I No Longer Want *Mind Your Money Activity 3*

Now grab fresh paper and write another list, this time focused on things you no longer want in your life. I left out 'don't' because the unconscious mind cannot process it. Again, be very clear, particularly if you have negative thoughts about any aspects of your life. Now is the time to get rid of all the 'stuff' holding you back. Really give this exercise thought; it has the power to reshape your future.

Things I No Longer Want in My Life
e.g. money worries

My version of this list included things like losing my habit for disorganisation and procrastination. Once you've finished, please grab your list along with some matches.

I suggest you take your list outside and burn it, making sure it's not fire season. Watch the list burn to a pile of ashes, taking your negative thoughts, energy and attitude with it. Then return the ashes to the earth, bury them in sand or dirt, so the earth can complete the cleansing process

Mind Your Money Tip

Be clear on what you want to achieve or attract into your life. Focus on what you want. Give no energy or thought to things that no longer serve you so you no longer attract them.

Chapter 3

Take Control

'Manage your wants so they do not get ahead of your needs.'
—Gayle McKew

Are spending habits making you wealthy or sabotaging your financial plans? Is what you're doing really working for you? Are you becoming wealthy? If you're not sure, or your answer is no, let's consider what's happening and who you *really* are making wealthy. If your answer is yes, read on because you could learn something to help you be wealthier.

Most of us have a dream to be wealthy, to retire early (right now would be good, right?) and to have a great lifestyle. Realistically, how far along are you towards creating your dream lifestyle? You might think you're working towards your goal because you go to work every day; yet your behaviours could be sabotaging your ideal outcome.

Financial sabotage

Is your money feeding a habit that sabotages your long-term financial plans? Be honest with yourself—are you self-sabotaging your financial goals? Or maybe you allow others to influence you, to sabotage your efforts through unplanned or unnecessary spending? *Of course not! Why would I do that?*

There are many ways people self-destruct financially. Let me ask, when you went shopping recently, either in store or online, did you let a good sale or great bargain get in the way of what you had planned to spend or even what you intended to buy? Maybe you bought something you hadn't planned on buying. Your capacity to sniff out a great bargain could be costing you in more ways than you planned.

It's easy to succumb to sabotaging behaviours and the influence of marketers. Financial sabotage comes in many forms, with many unaware of how much sabotage and damage we are, or have been, doing to our financial health.

Can you relate to any of these behaviours? Do you know someone who may:

* have all the latest toys, big screen TVs or electronic gadgets
* have the fastest, most impressive car they can afford to finance
* have just had the holiday of their dreams but will be paying it off for years
* regularly buy take-away coffee and food
* have an enviable selection of handbags and shoes
* be lazy when it comes to cooking, so they eat out more than they eat in
* have the best pay TV subscription money can buy even though there's no time to watch it
* smoke or regularly play Lotto or the lottery
* pay **only** the minimum off their credit card
* not pay off the entire credit card every month
* have multiple credit cards and use one to pay off the other?

The person you know like this has *a spending habit*, the strongest form of self-sabotage.

Here are a few more behaviours that strongly hint at a spending habit. They:

* spend more than planned on an item they 'need' (it's probably really a want)

* spend when bored, upset or angry
* buy something they don't need simply because it's on sale (a 'bargain') and looks good—*impulse buying* (either online or in-store)
* get into debt for something they simply can't afford and really don't need
* are addicted to spending
* gamble, including Lotto, lotteries, poker machines, cards, table games and so on
* habitually 'do' social spending (must have that coffee every day).

Who are you making wealthy?

You may have started to figure out who is being made wealthy here—it's not you! It's likely to be a retailer, bank or finance provider. By having a spending habit, avid spenders really are working hard on increasing the profits of the retailers, banks and finance companies. The shareholders of these same companies love consumers with spending habits, as they end up making the shareholders wealthy.

The CEO and shareholders of your favourite retailers, banks and finance companies love consumers with spending habits. I can almost hear them cheer as avid consumers enter a store. The businesses that get the greatest benefit from people's spending habits have an arsenal of tricks and temptations to keep consumers spending.

Let's consider some of their weapons:

* TV advertising and infomercials
* offering access to more credit to encourage consumers to spend more
* store promotions and credit providers offering 24, 36 or 48 month interest-free periods—often with no structured requirements to make repayments
* retailers allowing approved purchasers to buy now, with no immediate payments required, then to start paying for their spending in, say, three months' time
* clearance sales

- other in-store and online 'tricks', like bonus offers, to encourage consumers to buy.

If consuming is a habit, realise that while you might 'love' the thrill of spending, you are not helping your financial wellbeing. Of course retailers love consumers who spend; they rely on their money and their addiction to using credit, and consider spenders to be easy prey for their marketing team.

Parting consumers from their money is *the* sales objective for most retailers. It is *not* to provide consumers with a bargain or great value. Shop assistants are taught to apply some form of sales pressure—some barely discernible and some as subtle as a sledgehammer. It's up to you to be aware of this as you shop.

Think back to the last time you were in a fast food restaurant. Was the assistant 'kind' enough to ask, 'Would you like to upsize your meal?' or 'Would you like fries with that?'

'Sure', you agreed, thinking, *It's harmless, right? What difference could a few extra fries make? I can toss them out if I don't eat them.*

I have news for you—you lost that round of the shopping game, the store won. They sold more than you had intended to buy. You spent more money than planned and consumed a lot more calories than you really needed. You lost out in more ways than one on that transaction. What could you do now in a similar situation? Say 'no'. Stop letting your wants, or worse still someone else's wants (the store's), get ahead of your needs.

Stop letting your wants get ahead of your needs.

Take back control

I have to break it to you: If you intend on being successful, you are going to have to take control of your spending. Otherwise, if you change nothing, you will likely be headed for financial disaster. It's time to stop allowing others to benefit from your existing spending habits; it's your turn to benefit.

Let's consider your personal spending and figure out what *is* driving your negative habits. There are plenty of ways to have what you want and need. The key is:

Learn to be reasonable about managing your timing expectations.

You are the one who controls when you get whatever it is that you want or need. The success of how and when you reach your long-term goals is entirely up to you.

I'm not trying to be a kill-joy here, just pointing out facts. Finding balance and acting in a pre-planned way so that your long-term goals can be achieved, while also enjoying life in a smart way, are the *keys* to your success. A few of the negative behaviours and habits to avoid proactively are:

* trying to keep up with the Joneses
* marketing influences
* strong emotions such as anger or despair
* envy
* greed
* depression.

The most obvious damage can arise through *trying to 'keep up with the Joneses'*—those people you know who always have the latest toys and the best holidays. Overspending so that you can have the same things as the Joneses isn't smart and will end up damaging your long-term financial health.

Marketers work hard at sabotaging our spending; generally we are *not aware of the subtle influences marketers use to impact our buying habits*. Marketing arms of multi-national corporate organisations have huge budgets—all aimed at finding ways for you to spend your hard-earned income on buying their latest product. When you buy *without a real need*, you've succumbed to their marketing hype and they've clearly won that round of the marketing battle.

Personal drivers can cause sabotage, like how *we spend when we are being impacted by strong emotions such as anger or despair.* The person with the most purchases at the end of the day doesn't always win. Usually the merchant or a credit provider is the winner, particularly where there is uncontrolled and excessive shopping driven by out-of control-emotions.

Additional emotional risks include envy and greed; both lead to emotionally driven overspending, which you end up being unable to afford. Sadly, depression is yet another driver of ill-considered spending. Many times people will try to fill emotional voids temporarily by spending. Delivery of the anticipated item provides a short-term positive emotional surge, yet it's often followed by even more despair and related financial turmoil.

Let's consider spending behaviours and the drivers behind the decision to succumb to the temptations of a bargain; a bargain that will sabotage financial goals. If we're honest, we sometimes get to the point where we simply can't seem to help ourselves. Well, no more. It's time to adopt some positive behaviour and practise smart shopping.

Challenge yourself not to spend!

Not only will it help your budget and overall financial situation, it's also an exercise in personal control. I recently implemented a personal challenge to buy only items I need, like food, fuel, undies and health services. I've challenged myself not to buy new outer clothing or shoes for a whole year—so far I'm going really well. I keep receiving tempting emails with fantastic discounts on offer. I've found myself deleting emails and unsubscribing from lots of distribution lists. I'm already feeling the benefits of spring cleaning my email box; not only am I gaining time not spending for the sake of reacting to their marketing efforts, it is also super satisfying.

If you manage not to spend, or to at least redirect spending to something you *really need,* rather than buying something you merely want, you're making big steps towards your goals. Congratulations. You're moving towards your end game and your big goals.

Money saving tactics

In this section I'm going to encourage you to practise the craft of using money saving tactics when buying, rather than self-sabotaging through bad spending habits, like shopping for the sake of shopping. You need to be smart about how and where you spend your money and why.

Only buy things you need

The dress for that function is 'to die for'. It's got an $800 price tag; your budget is $300. The shop assistant says you look amazing, and you've swallowed the bait and willingly spent the money.

You're going to be paying for that rash decision for a long time, particularly if you used credit and don't pay your credit card off every month. If you pay the minimum every month, you could still be paying for that dress in ten years, long after the dress is in land fill!

What options do you have? Continue shopping until you find something in your price range, perhaps a pre-loved (second-hand) option? You won't see someone else in the same outfit. Pre-loved outlets offer great bargain shopping while often allowing you to support a charity of your choice at the same time. Win-win!

Avoid spending because you're bored, depressed, upset or angry

I remember how it felt to be in the middle of an emotionally-driven spending spree—where you don't care, you're blisteringly angry and spending is soothing your emotions.

Who really pays the cost when you finish taking your angst out on your credit card? Last time I checked, it wasn't the person or situation that got me angry enough to go shopping in the first place. The bill goes to the angry spender.

I admit I've been guilty of emotional spending in the past, until I figured out the only one being hurt by the spending was me! Now I avoid shopping when I'm angry, bored or upset as I'm *very* aware that I can be swayed to spend more than I need on items I don't need, all driven by strong and destructive emotions.

So, what can you do instead? Deal with boredom or upset emotions in other ways; go for a walk or a run, start singing at the top of your lungs (this is one of my favourites, even though I'm often out of tune and have been recently told not to give up my day job by someone who heard me murdering a tune). How can you stay angry when belting out your favourite song? I can't!

If we're being grown up about it, try resolving the issue with anyone who has contributed to your mood. Not only is this a great release, it helps you to stop giving your personal power away.

Avoid succumbing to impulse buying

There's nothing wrong with a good bargain, providing you are going to use the item soon (say, within the next month) and it's an item of necessity—think food or clothing. If it's not a necessity, all you've done is move the shopkeeper's surplus and unwanted stock to your place *and* you've paid them for the privilege.

Something that sits in your cupboard, unused for years, is not a bargain—it's a clear waste of money! Do you know anyone who might have a multitude of expensive 'mistakes' hidden in the back of a cupboard? Think of the people you know who've spent money during an emotionally-driven spending spree and lived to regret it!

I appreciate it's possible to get a buzz from a good bargain, but there needs to be limits to spending. Some suffer from a shopping obsession or addiction; it's important for these people to take time to review what's really driving their unhappiness before they press the 'buy' button and create a deeper financial black hole. Please, please avoid this type of self-destructive habit; nobody can afford this type of behaviour.

Remember ... your money is a retailer's sales target. Ask yourself ...

Will this purchase bring me closer to my goal or further from it?

* * *

Ask yourself: Can I afford it?

Think long and hard about getting into debt for something that you simply can't afford and really do not need. I know people with boxes of outdated, yet still highly usable, electronic equipment and gadgets gathering dust in the garage. Their new purchases are sitting in pride of place where others can see them in use, hoping to trigger gadget envy.

They haven't finished paying for the items that are gathering dust, and there are now new toys to pay for as well. Do you suffer gadget envy? Why are you even considering buying it when you simply can't afford it? Ask yourself:

* Do I have an immediate need for it?
* Is the purchase in line with my end goals?
* Do I simply want it?

If you're not sure of the answers, why not delay for a day—or even three? Even if you're already at the store, leave before you are tempted to spend; you can always come back later if you need to. Three little words can also help contain spending:

* Stop
* Think
* Save

* * *

We've talked about creating your ideal life and images to support the feelings you get when you know you've achieved your goals. You've done great work so far. I hope you're happy with yourself; you're doing well. That lovely warm feeling you get when things are going well and you are happy with yourself, can you connect with it? It feels good, right? That is your feeling of success!

Next time you can't make up your mind about spending on a big item or consider something that is going to blow the budget big time, *before you decide* I want you to reconnect to the feeling 'success' brings. Why? Because if you're feeling success because you're on track, you will not like the feeling you get when you *know* you are about to sabotage yourself. Ask yourself, 'Will the purchase bring me closer to achieving my goal or will it take me further from it?'

If the answer is 'further from', consider how *not* buying the item will make you feel when you actually achieve your goal.

You will be in control, not left regretting the purchase. Can you feel the difference?

My final suggestion on this topic is to practise a few words and phrases like these:

* No, thank you!
* I'll think about it and get back to you.

If you're getting a quote from a service provider, you can say things like:

* I have a rule to get three quotes before I make a decision; so I'll get back to you.
* I will give you an answer in three days' time.

Why three days? It's a long enough time for you to emotionally detach yourself from any influence by the supplier or retailer.

New habits cost less

I remember a meeting with a client who was an avid spender. Her husband was an avid saver, so her spending habits were creating serious relationship tensions. She was explaining the importance of some of her recent purchases including her sense of entitlement to spend. 'I work, I should be able to spend what I like', was what she kept telling her hubby. She was unaware of the impact of the situation, yet her husband was ready to start all-out warfare over the spending habit.

I was absolutely exasperated, she was completely ignoring the advice they were paying to access; advice focused on paying off their personal debts and building an investment portfolio, to allow an early retirement. Yet she kept derailing their long-term goals with her spending habits.

We discussed cutting up the credit card, but she wasn't ready to give it up. In absolute frustration we came up with the plan to '*put her card on ice'*—literally. It was the only way we could think of to slow down her spending. This is how we did it:

How How to put a card 'on ice'

We half-filled a plastic ice-cream container with water and froze it. We then placed her card on the ice before filling the remainder of the container with water and freezing that too. If she needed to use her card, she agreed to defrost the ice block containing her card at room temperature. Defrosting in the microwave would damage the card; she needed to wait for nature to take its course

It gave her time to assess whether the intended purchase was needed and it give her enough emotional space and time to bring the long-term plan to the front of her mind. It worked a treat, one spending habit broken. Yippee! Hopefully, you won't need to be this drastic with yourself.

Smoking and gambling your money away?

It would be remiss of me not to discuss this. Not only can smoking damage your health, it damages your finances as well. Consider what your smoking habit costs over a year. If you spend just $30 per week on smoking, it turns into $1560 each year going up in smoke. Just imagine you're spending $100 per week—that's an astonishing $5200 per year disappearing. What could you do with that money if you harnessed it? Let's not forget the saved costs in medical bills later on in life from years of smoking. If you need help to quit, the money spent on some patches or therapy will be far less than the costs of cigarettes in the long run.

Cost-effective replacement habits can include chomping on carrot or celery sticks if you need to put something in your mouth. A bunch of celery or a kilo of carrots will go a long way and cost way less than your smoking habit does each week. Brush your teeth, the flavour may chase away the craving plus you will have a winning, white smile.

Better yet, get to the bottom of the habit. Dig deep enough within your psyche so that you understand what's driving that damn habit. Is it stress or something else emotionally driven? If it's stress, please do yourself and everyone that loves you a favour and find a more healthy way to minimise your stress or emotional issues.

Gambling, in any form—Lotto, lotteries, poker machines, cards, table games—is a waste of money. The probability of winning the Saturday Lotto in Australia is extremely remote, the table below shows how remote.[8]

Division	Winning Numbers Required	Probability (Single Game)
1st Division	6	1 in 8 145 060
2nd Division	5 + supplementary	1 in 678 755

As a regular Lotto, lottery or other game-of-chance player, you may as well throw your money in the air and watch it fly away.

Social habits

Do you regularly eat and drink out or get take-away? Mmm coffee… You love coffee and have at least two cups a day and know the barista's first name. It's great to catch up with friends over lunch; you're more than happy to eat lunch out every day. Better yet, let's stop off for a drink after work to catch up with friends.

8 www.en.wikipedia.org/wiki/Lotteries_in_Australia

How much are those social habits costing each week? Most people never stop to consider the cost; they're too busy having fun and catching up on the latest gossip.

What do your habits cost? Let's start with the coffee habit. If each cup costs $4.50 and you average two cups a day, seven days a week, 52 weeks a year, this habit will cost you at least $3276 per annum.

Social Spending (based on two drinks per day)	Average daily cost	Weekly average cost	Annual average cost
Coffee	$9.00	$63.00	$3276.00
after work—House wine/beer* on	$10.00	$30.00	$1560.00
Drinks after work—upmarket wine*	$30.00	$90.00	$4680.00
Drinks after work—upmarket beer*	$20.00	$60.00	$3120.00
Drinks after work—Cocktails*	$50.00	$150.00	$7800.00
Lunch daily	$20.00	$140.00	$7280.00

*Drinks after work, three nights per week

What's your tipple—wine, beer or cocktails? Let's say a house beer is $5 and wine about the same. If you're drinking at an upmarket bar, a beer could be $10 and a wine about $15 through to a cocktail running from $20 to $25 per glass.

Assuming you have two drinks a night, your spending could be from $10 to $50, depending on where you drink and what you're drinking. But if you have four drinks per night, your nightly spend could be anywhere from $20 to $100. You may not go drinking every night, but three times a week could see you spend anywhere from $30 to $300. Your yearly spend could be anywhere from $1560 to $15 600 per annum.

With just coffee and drinking habits you could be spending anywhere between $4485 and $18 885 each year. We haven't even included your lunching out habit, which could be costing you an average of $20 per day or an extra $7300 per annum.

Social spending could be costing anywhere from $11 785 to $26 185 each year. Enough to buy a car or even go a long way towards building a deposit for a property purchase—and that's only in the first year! Imagine the impact over many years. It's mind boggling.

Have you ever added up the cost of socialising before? By simply making a few small changes to your habits, you will save a small fortune annually. Have a go at making small changes such as:

* bringing lunch from home most days instead of eating out every day
* reducing your coffee and drinking habits
* socialising at home rather than out on the town
* having a barbecue or a dinner party where everyone brings a dish to share the cost of entertaining.

Be loyal to you

Loyalty is a valued commodity … although loyalty can be frequently misplaced and not always deserved. I am exceptionally loyal to family and friends—those I trust.

I refuse to extend loyalty to an organisation though, especially organisations that don't care about the impact on me and my finances. Organisations only care about their own profitability and their corporate bottom line.

Are you loyal to a bank, telecommunications provider, internet provider, utilities provider or insurer? Do you know what the cost is to you? You really could be in for a nasty surprise when it comes to the real cost of your loyalty.

I can understand brand loyalty if you are a majority shareholder in a particular company. Unless you're a majority shareholder, it's time to consider where you get the best value for the money you spend. Stop spending blindly.

Do what your bank says? I think not!

I worked in banking for many years and know most people, when faced with a financial decision, go to their bank. Friendly staff will listen to your needs and suggest *the* most suitable product available. The solution offered may not be the best fit for your needs, yet it's the only one available. You agree to buy the product simply because it's sold by your bank and is convenient.

By being loyal to your bank, you will not get the best outcome for you. The best outcome, the sale of a product, went to your bank; whereas a little time spent doing some serious shopping around could have saved you quite a bit of money and provided you with a much better outcome. It's time for discernment and objectivity.

You've improved the bank's bottom line. The smarter strategy would be to look at products from a range of providers to find the one that suits your needs. I'll tell you how to do this sort of shopping around without having to do the footwork soon.

Most of us have to eat, pay rent or pay a mortgage; bills for the utilities, phone, internet, and insurances for your assets and your life keep coming. Do you sometimes feel like you are working just to pay your bills?

Electricity bills seem to go up every year at a rate much higher than inflation. Try to reduce usage where possible; turn lights off and use energy saving bulbs. We even have solar hot water and solar panels on the roof. Despite all of our tactics, the base cost of electricity keeps marching higher and higher.

In most houses big bills cause financial chaos and despair. Some only complain; the trick is to find cheaper alternative providers. *Start shopping around for better deals*.

My home and contents insurance bill made me shop around recently. There had been a 25% increase in premium costs; a rise that largely hadn't been planned for. A letter explained the rise was linked to a string of natural disaster-related claims.

I spoke with an insurance broker; I wanted a suitable alternative replacement cover. The professional shopped around; all the quotes were more expensive. Replacement policies were at least 14% more expensive than the actual premium I had to pay.

By checking, I knew we had the best price.

No more convenience shopping

How much is convenience shopping costing you? It's a legitimate concern if your actions and habits are costing you a great deal of money each week.

Let me explain how, by implementing alternative habits, you could save a bundle of money.

Even if you're a single person, I know you will need to eat. The last time I checked, there was a simple equation:

{(Eating = need for food = cost) x multiple people} = MEGA cost

How and where you shop determines the *cost* and the *MEGA cost* portion of the equation.

At fast food restaurants you pay for the convenience of having someone else prepare food and serve it. Plus, if you decide to eat out you don't have to clean up after yourself. Yet if you put some effort into preparing your meals, you can feed yourself better and for a lot less than you would pay at a fast food restaurant. Yet how many times do we choose convenience over saving money? It all adds up.

At convenience chain stores, we willingly pay more at the check-out for the convenience of proximity and the knowledge we can access hours than you would if you were to buy the same items at the supermarket. Sometimes paying for convenience is worth it, yet it can turn out to be far more expensive than you think. A little bit of planning could make a huge difference to your budget.

* * *

Let's have a look at the effect of two different types of shopping for a family of six adults.

Shopper One will only shop at the local big name supermarket. This habit is based entirely on convenience; it's a five-minute drive from her home. She buys well-known brands and, *for her convenience*, includes lots of *remove-from-the-box-and-heat-in-the-oven* items. She buys everything (meat, vegetables and other food items) in the one store. As a result of her shopping habits, she pays top dollar for every item that goes into her shopping trolley because she shops for convenience.

She feeds a family of six adults (who are fussy eaters with small appetites) and one small dog for around $520 per week.

Shopper Two is willing to drive up to ten minutes from home and even to make a couple of stops to get better value for her spend. This sees her visit the local butcher, the fresh produce markets and a discount grocery chain.

This family prefers a varied and fresh diet. It's freshly prepared foods rather than packaged foods; the cost of convenience is kept low.

With a little bit of effort, Shopper Two is able to feed a family of six adults with good appetites on $380 per week.

Doing the sums

Let's look at the average cost per adult only:

Family of six	Cost per person per week	Weekly cost	Annualised cost (rounded)
Shopper One	$86.66	$520.00	$27 040.00
Shopper Two	$63.33	$380.00	$19 760.00
Shopper Two savings compared to Shopper One			$ 7280.00
Ten year saving			$72 800.00

For Shopper One, it's $86.66 per person. For Shopper Two it's $63.33. That's an amazing $23.33 per person per week difference in spending.

While it doesn't sound much, let's look at the multiplier effect over time.

Let's calculate the annual cost of living for each household for grocery-related items.

* Shopper One spends: {($86.66 x 6) x 52 weeks} = $27 038 p.a.
* Shopper Two spends: {($63.33 x 6) x 52 weeks} = $19 759 p.a.
* Difference in spending: ($27 038–$19 759) = $7279 p.a.

By changing shopping habits there is potential for Shopper One to save thousands each year. What could you do with an extra $7279 each year?

Over ten years imagine saving in excess of $72 000. Think about what you could do with that!

* * *

The recommendations I've made in this chapter are to make small changes to your spending and socialising habits. The changes aren't meant to destroy your lifestyle, but to encourage you to adapt a little so your finances aren't destroyed by your social life. Making choices to support your long-term financial health will ensure your future lifestyle goals can be met. Consider the potential difference you can make to your future.

Do you remember I banged on about the importance of a budget and that you might need to revisit your budget if you were overspending, in the *Foundation* chapter? Now would be a great time to revisit your budget. You're aware of some habits that might have been taking you off track and now you know ways to make savings in those areas.

What have you got to lose? Not a thing. On the other hand, what is there to gain from making small changes? Plenty! The effort will be worth it. By making those changes you're putting yourself back in the driver's seat.

The purpose is not to judge; it's to raise awareness of potential problems. I know some habits are hard to change, yet changes can be achieved if you are willing and determined.

You're likely reading this book because you're ready to change your financial position. Life's so much easier when the way you use money is positive; when your budget is running in the black and not in the red you're earning more than you're spending. Great work!

Have a really good look at your spending habits. Be honest; no more pussy footing around.

Change what you're doing or your results will stay the same.

* * *

Let's recap on some **positive spending habits** you can now adopt:

* Keep to your budget.
* Spend only when you're in a positive frame of mind, not suffering negative emotions.
* Plan and research your purchases.
* Only buy what you can need and can afford.
* Create new habits that cost less (e.g. quit smoking).
* Ditch any misplaced loyalty you have to brands and providers.
* Research your telephone and utilities suppliers and get on a better plan where possible.
* Buy less packaged, pre-cooked or take-away foods.
* Research where you can buy groceries at cheaper prices.

Your success in implementing all these money saving tactics will depend on your new beliefs. I'm going to give you an extra hand here with this, so you don't slip back into old behaviours.

There's a unique way of thinking you can adopt: Start thinking like an entrepreneur in relation to your finances. Start making decisions in a more business-focused manner. Decisions will be made for financial benefit *not* based on emotions. Let's have a look at that in more depth in the next chapter.

Mind Your Money Tip

Three little words can help contain spending: Stop—Think—Save.

Every time you buy something, regardless of how you pay, you are making a financial decision.

Chapter 4

Think, Plan and Walk Like an Entrepreneur

'I like thinking big. If you're going to be thinking anything, you might as well think big.'

— Donald Trump[9]

People like Richard Branson, Bill Gates and Oprah Winfrey think and act differently to most people. They're entrepreneurs—we need to learn to think like they do!

Entrepreneurship is a process of identifying and starting a business venture, sourcing and organising the required resources and taking both the risks and rewards associated with the venture.[10] Branson, Gates and Winfrey have each embraced this process many times over. It's not only they who receive the benefits; these people make positive impacts on the daily lives of many others through the capacity of their business operations to employ people, and of course through their products and services.

Thinking like an entrepreneur means connecting to creativity and a determination to identify and act on opportunities.

9 www.entrepreneur.com/article/241140

10 www.en.wikipedia.org/wiki/Entrepreneurship

We love the stories of those entrepreneurs who start from nothing and create amazing things. There's nothing to say you can't start something amazing too, particularly when it comes to your finances. I encourage you to start thinking and acting like an entrepreneur when it comes to your finances—think spiritual entrepreneur if it resonates better with your value system. Start thinking like an entrepreneur and you'll benefit in the long run.

Thinking like an entrepreneur means connecting to creativity and a determination to identify and act on opportunities. Most entrepreneurs are willing to step out of their comfort zone to achieve their end game. They keep adapting to challenges and will do what it takes to fulfil their dream. It's a big game that entrepreneurs play, full of action and determination, coupled with the need to make tough decisions to achieve their dreams. Are you willing to do whatever it takes to create your dream? If you're seeking financial success, it is worth stepping into the entrepreneurial mindset.

Begin your entrepreneurial journey by *identifying opportunities* to make positive changes and *start to treat your finances as if you are running a business*. It's time for you to begin sourcing knowledge and organising your resources (control your spending, investing and savings) so that you're able to take advantage of opportunities as they come your way.

Your actions will determine just how many rewards you get for the work you put in and the risks you will take in operating your 'business'—the business of managing your financial future. Are there parts of your 'business' life that might benefit from outsourcing? The first parts of your 'business' life that I can think of outsourcing are your bookwork, if you run a business, and your taxes, regardless of whether you are self-employed or an employee.

Do you think Branson and Co. do all of the hard work themselves? No way! They have other people to do the work—experts in specific areas—while they continue to take advantage of opportunities that come their way. Think like the big players if you want similar results.

Start by giving your 'business' a name, it can help to take the emotional attachment away from 'business' related decisions, particularly the tough ones you really may not want to make. While this concept sounds a little crazy, most people will work on their 'business' to ensure it is profitable and that costs are contained. Whereas people usually won't work on their personal 'stuff' because it's too uncomfortable and close to home.

Individuals who accumulate wealth see and use money differently than their peers. Wealth creators have *control over decisions* and *work with clear intentions and purpose*—just like a business owner does. They have plans for how to use their money as a tool for leverage (more on leverage later). Money allows them to invest in property and share portfolios—things that have *potential to make even more money* with little or no physical effort required.

A person of an entrepreneurial spirit will, as a general rule, look to take advantage of opportunities to get out of thankless and tedious work; they outsource the 'stuff' they hate or find boring. They realise the power of focusing their time on money-making activities and of investing in both property and share portfolios; realising that both investment types can provide regular income in the form of rent or dividends to the owner of the investment, as well as potential for an increase in value over time. It truly is a case of money making money.

Entrepreneurs capitalise on any investment income created as a result of investing. They know it can be harnessed to do whatever they like, which usually is to make even more money. They know investments can provide income to live on or to assist in extinguishing (paying off) debt. With shares and managed fund investments (in simple terms this is a pool of shares you can own part of), any income earned can be reinvested to buy more of those same income producing assets. It's a bit like having your cake and eating it too, only without the calories.

Are you starting to understand the power of thinking and acting like an entrepreneur yet?

Entrepreneurs know that if they want to have increased financial freedom, they need to have a range of income streams to fund their lifestyle. If you're seeking financial freedom, it's time to start thinking about having additional income streams other than your regular salary. If you want greater financial freedom and choices in the future, you need to start doing something about creating extra income now. The more income you have coming in, the more choices and opportunities you will be able to take advantage of.

Imagine more choices regarding:

* lifestyle—where and how you holiday or live
* how your children are educated
* when you can choose to become your own boss
* retiring when you can afford to, rather than when you have to.

Are those choices attractive? On the other hand, where there is no thought of using money to create personal advantages we can expect to be dealt the same boring stuff every week. Your boss makes decisions about your financial situation, like whether you earn an income or not, and how much they're willing to pay for your skills and services. Things will be out of your control.

Without the correct mindset, it's hard to appreciate the consequences of not making powerful and informed decisions for your future. People who rely on others usually are not making powerful decisions. Are you making powerful decisions?

People with entrepreneurial mindsets can be patient and are willing to wait for gratification or personal rewards. Oh, I'm not saying that Branson, Oprah and Co. don't have comfortable (okay affluent) lifestyles; what I am saying is that they didn't spend excessive money on lifestyle *until they were in a position to afford it ...* they waited.

In reality, most people who have lots of lifestyle 'toys' (cars, holidays, jet skis or even that amazing shoe and handbag collection) who have a pile of personal debt. It's worth considering that even though their 'toy' boxes are full to overflowing, they really don't have a great relationship with money. They do have great relationships with credit providers who continue to provide credit for items that will eventually be worthless. These people often have lots of debt with no real assets to show for it. Clearly they think as consumers with no consideration for the future. What a contrast.

Does avid consumerism sound familiar? It's time to prioritise and become empowered in the way in which you handle money. What have you got to lose other than years of working drudgery? Implementing changes now could mean that you won't be working just to keep the banks happy and their shareholders rich. You will be working for your future.

Imagine a life of choices and eventual financial freedom. With some effective decision making it can be yours!

Plan, plan, plan your goals!

Allocate yourself enough time so you can sit down uninterrupted for at least an hour and begin listing your 'business' goals. If you aren't sure of your business goals, take as long as you need. Most people need anywhere from three hours to a whole day to develop the initial plan for a business.

Your initial plan is simply a starting point and will need to be tweaked and worked on to allow you to understand the actions you need to take for your 'business' to be successful enough for you to reach your 'business' goals.

You need to know what your goals are *first;* otherwise you're going to bumble around not knowing whether you've ever achieved your goals. Bumbling isn't rewarding; achieving something measurable is.

Create a strategy

You need to know how you are going to achieve those 'business' goals; planning alone won't work. The next step is to create a strategy, including a list of actions to take to bring you closer to your goal.

As we're talking about your 'business' it's time to take a long hard look at your expenditure. You need to consider things like:

Is the cost essential to your 'business' operation? If not why are you spending money on the item?
Is the cost excessive for what you are receiving? Sometimes a small change to your essential spending habits can save you a small fortune over time. Ask yourself if you are buying brand names you really can't afford or if you are buying more than you need.

There's a trend towards online food shopping, and my friends who use this service say it saves them a fortune because even though they pay a delivery fee, they aren't tempted by treats as they wander the aisles of the store. I use a vegetable delivery service and find the service is saving me heaps, both money and time, as I no longer buy what I think my tastebuds 'want' at the market. Now we eat what's in season and has been delivered.

Is there a cheaper alternative? Sometimes all it takes to find out is a quick comparison shop online. Our habits mean we use the same supplier, yet that habit could end up costing us more than we had planned. Changing habits gives us a chance to buy essential 'business' equipment at potentially discounted prices, meaning our financial bottom line benefits.

Can the cost be reduced in any way? Business owners always consider options to trim costs. Could your 'business' benefit from trimming costs too? Consider the services you regularly use like phone, internet, electricity and insurances (home, car and personal). Next time a bill for one of these lobs into your mail box, stop and do a little bit of research *before* you pay the bill.

Phone, internet and electricity services are often on a contract basis. Check when your contract is getting close to ending. Start researching your options as there are often deals available if you are willing to switch providers.

For example, I know there are a range of options available that will save considerable cost to my 'business' for phones, and it is my intention to transfer to a pre-paid option when my contract is up. Why? I stand to save around half of my monthly costs when compared to being on a post-paid contract.

Additionally, electricity and telecommunication providers are often able to provide incentives if you are willing to switch. You might suffer a small amount of work or inconvenience while the switch happens, but then your 'business' will benefit from the serious savings available. The effort you take will be rewarded with savings.

Is the cost associated with the creation of income? If so, you *still* need to apply all of the above tests to these costs. Only if this cost is used to create income can you prioritise it above all of your other 'business' costs because those other costs are not making your 'business' money.

Make it measurable

When you are planning your goals, make sure each goal is measurable in some way. Put an amount and a date on a goal so your success in achieving it can be measured in specific terms. Wishy-washy goals are just wishes and cannot be measured, so you have no way of knowing if they have been achieved.

Let's look at some examples of specific goals.

Goal: Reduce costs—By the end of September *this year* you plan to have taken specific steps to reduce your costs by 5% compared to last year's costs. This means if your costs were say $25 000 last year, your costs will need to decrease by $1250 to $23 750 this year. This goal is both specific and measurable

Goal: Holiday at end of year—You name an amount you have to save by a certain date so that you can enjoy a week at a resort in Fiji in November *this year*. You discover packages are available from $700 for flights and accommodation, plus you will need spending money. So you need at least $1500 for your holiday but would prefer to have some more money available so you can do some exciting tourist stuff. You set your goal at $2500, with 50% of the package costs being needed in a month to secure the flight and accommodation at the sale price.

Goal: Buy a new property—You have done some research and you think you will need to spend up to $375 000 to buy a new property. This means you need to have at least $18,750 available as a deposit, plus almost $5400 to cover stamp duty if you are buying your home in Queensland (each state is different) and are not a first home owner. Legal costs could be as much as $2000. You've figured out your savings goal is $26 150. Now they're both measurable and specific—tick! The timeframe is up to you because it will depend entirely on your income and savings capacity.

Goal: Pay off your debts—You decide how long it will take to clear your existing debt; if you concentrate, you can pay off your credit card in 6 months—tick—measurable and specific.

Steps to buying a property

Do you know the steps you need to take to buy a property? Most people have no idea. Let's look at some of the basics. It's definitely not an exhaustive list; just a broad brush approach to give you an idea of some of the things you need to consider to reach this goal.

* Your current savings. Do you have any? You're going to need at least a 5% deposit, relative to the amount you intend to spend, and enough other money to cover things like stamp duty, legal costs and pest and building inspections.
* Existing loans or debts; your future lender will look at how well you've been paying back these loans and whether you can afford to take on more debt.
* Check your capacity to borrow to be sure it's in line with your proposed budget. This step is important as it will allow you to assess whether you can afford to make the loan repayments *before* you go to the bother of applying for a loan.
* You need loan approval so you know you can access the funds you need to meet your goal of buying a house a reality.
* You need to find the home of your dreams, of course being sure to stay within your budget.

Making 'business' decisions

When making a buying decision, think like a business person. Is the item you are considering buying a want or a need? Will it improve your 'business' by streamlining your operation or can the 'business' operate effectively without it? Will the purchase bring you closer to your end goal and contribute to your 'business' model? Will it sabotage your budget or plans? Because you are treating your money as a business, what you're buying should add value to your 'business' and its bottom line.

We've looked at the importance of having an entrepreneurial mindset that works *for you* rather than against you. We've cleared away some of what is not serving you and encouraged you to think like an entrepreneur. The challenge is for you to begin applying those new skills to your 'business'—the business of managing your money. The money-hungry tactics of the big corporates are exposed next; you'll learn how to protect yourself from the financial damage they cause.

Over many years of working in banks and operating as a lending representative, I've seen lots of people 'accidentally' become overcommitted financially to the number and size of loans they've taken out over time.

Credit is relatively easy to gain these days, and each loan comes with a loan contract big enough to overwhelm and confuse people. Experience shows most borrowers don't read the contract they sign. As a result many have no real understanding of the obligations they agree to by signing the contract.

It's easy for important stuff to be overlooked in the excitement of getting your loan approved and buying 'stuff'. Sadly, overlooking important things can lead to financial chaos. Let's look at what managing or mismanaging your credit obligations can mean to you.

Mind Your Money Tip

Start treating your money as a business and take the emotion out of financial decision making.

Part 2

TAKING CARE OF BUSINESS

Chapter 6

Good Debt—Bad Debt

'Debt is one person's liability, but another person's asset.'

—Paul Krugman[11]

Debt is debt, isn't it? There are subtle but important differences to be aware of when choosing the type of debt you elect to take on.

It's almost impossible to live debt-free these days. Most of us simply aren't in a position to pay cash for our homes, cars or even our children's education.

Think of how many bills you receive; chances are more than a few are appearing each week. *The total of those bills and the loans you owe is the amount of credit that has been extended to you by a range of providers.* Most people have accessed quite a lot of credit without thinking about it. With the availability of easy credit, too many of us have access to too much debt to comfortably handle; sometimes it gets out of hand.

Years ago, there used to be a lending policy that assessed credit worthiness when buying a home. The policy restricted the portion of your income that could be used to repay debt, with the idea of protecting

11 www.brainyquote.com/quotes/quotes/p/paulkrugma439843.html?src=t_debt

both the lender and borrower; the lender from default (not paying) by the borrower and the borrower from over-commitment (not being able to afford repayments). At that time, the portion of the borrower's gross income used to service (repay) long-term debt payments, including your mortgage and credit cards, could not exceed 32%. While it was a conservative measure, it meant people were in a position to repay any debts they incurred easily.

Now those safe guards, for lenders and borrowers alike, simply don't appear to be there. Credit has become freely available and now, as long as you can continue to meet the repayments, credit providers don't really care about the impact of your borrowings on other sections of your life; they're too busy thinking of their bottom line, not yours.

Good debt

Of course, avoiding debt at any cost is not always smart either, particularly if it means depleting cash reserves you have for emergencies—we talked about this in *Foundation*: *Financial Check-up*. The challenge is learning to judge which debts could be beneficial and work towards bringing you closer to your goals, and which ones will take you away from your goals. More importantly, it's about managing the money you do elect to borrow wisely.

Good debt includes borrowing for anything you need (not want), but can't afford to pay for up front, without wiping out cash reserves or liquidating all your investments. Generally, we consider this to include buying a home to live in and even a modest car. However, is it really good debt?

Good debt relates to buying assets that provide income and potential for capital appreciation during the period the asset is held (owned). In Australia, buying an investment property or investment portfolio using borrowed money is often considered to be a great example of good debt. This is primarily because the Australian Tax Office currently provides tax concessions and allows deductions relating to the cost of holding the asset, including costs of insurances, maintenance and interest relating to the purchase of assets. The Australian Tax Office allows deductions where there is potential for a related income stream to be generated by the purchased asset.

Where debt makes sense, only take loans you can afford to meet monthly payments on comfortably. Even excessive 'good' borrowing can be asking for trouble, particularly if you aren't able to manage the long-term repayments.

Bad debt

Bad debt includes loans you've taken out for things you didn't need and really can't afford. Lifestyle 'things' you put on your credit card is bad debt.

All the things you've purchased on your credit card: the holiday you're still paying for, the meals, the cinema or stage show. Other than having a great time, did you realise all that spending on your lifestyle has likely created a pile of bad debt?

I've seen lots of cases where people were juggling multiple credit cards; the worst case was six credit cards right to the maximum of their credit limits. Can you imagine how you would feel if you had more than $70 000 worth of credit card debt and end up with nothing to show for all that spending? I saw a couple struggling with juggling four credit cards and wanting to buy a house. The sad thing was they had absolutely nothing to show for the debt other than having had a really great lifestyle and a very hungry horse eating them into masses of debt. Because of their credit card debt level, not one lender would consider giving them a loan to buy a property; their habits had derailed their ambitions, goals and dreams.

Cards—good, bad and ugly

In my opinion, the worst form of debt is credit card debt, particularly as there are usually no related 'assets' to show for all the spending. 'Assets' are items with a saleable value; so effectively they are something to show for your expenditure.

When assessing loans, credit-card interest is charged at the highest interest rate in the market place, particularly when the rate is compared to a personal loan or home loan.

It's far too easy to spend more than you can afford when you pay by credit card instead of using cash. With cash you can only spend what's in your account; a credit card allows you to spend to the account limit.

A quick check of the Australian Securities and Investments Commission's (ASIC's) Money Smart website shows there is an average of $4700 of outstanding credit card debt for every card holder in Australia.[12]

Sadly, this statistic means each card holder is expected to pay in excess of $800 per annum in interest charges, assuming interest rates applicable are between 15–20% per annum . I'm sure you have better things to do with $800 per year than to pay it to your credit provider.

There are times when the use of a credit card for your monthly spending can be advantageous; *however*, there can be big problems if you get it wrong. I use a credit card for most household expenses; each and every month the balance is paid off in full. It allows me to use the credit card company's money for a whole month without any cost. The key to this strategy is discipline; otherwise, it's possible to end up with excessive debt where interest is charged at the highest interest rate possible because there is excess debt sitting unpaid on your credit card.

Interest-free

You've seen lots of television and media advertising encouraging us to *buy now, pay later* or *buy now, no repayments required until...* These offers of finance are generally extended on the basis of an unsecured credit card. While these offers can be great and particularly helpful when managed effectively, they can be a disaster for the unwary, particularly if used badly and not repaid by the due date.

These apparently generous credit providers frequently charge in the order of 30% per annum for unsecured credit card borrowings.

---

12 www.moneysmart.gov.au/borrowing-and-credit/credit-cards/credit-card-debt-clock as at 3rd March 2013

Unsuspecting people don't read the fine print and they don't start to repay the debt until they're forced to by the credit provider.

This is where the sting of high interest penalties kicks in. When the debt isn't repaid in full by the end of the interest-free period, *the provider goes right back to the date of purchase and starts charging you interest* until the debt is repaid. The offer of easy credit may not sound too bad to some; it gets us what we want when we want it. Yet let's imagine I've purchased a new flat-screen television for $1000 using one of those cards that offer a 24 month no-interest, no-repayment credit term. There is also a fee of $5 per month on the account.

If I am smart, I will ensure the amount is repaid in full by the time the 24 months interest-free term is complete. I can calculate that $1000 ÷ 24 = $41.67, which needs to be repaid or saved each month, along with the $5 monthly fee. So I will have to either:

* save $1120 in an account ready to repay the debt in full prior to the 24 months interest-free period lapsing or
* if I couldn't trust myself to save, I could choose to pay $46.67 per month off the debt.

Either option would ensure no interest was payable on the initial debt, providing the perfect outcome to the scenario—not one cent of interest paid. You're winning!

If I did no planning, I would only have to start to repay the minimum repayment when the credit provider told me to. According to the ASIC Money Smart website, I will still be paying for the item in around 28 years' time. The initial $1000 television will have cost me in excess of $5000. Plus, the television will long ago have been despatched to land fill.

Justification to borrow

Sometimes, the decision to borrow doesn't hinge on how much cash you have available but on whether there are ways to make your money work harder for you than the actual cost of borrowing money. You have to ask if you can get a better return by leaving your investments intact and borrowing money instead. In some, but not all cases, you can; other times it can turn into a disaster.

If interest rates are low, compare what you'll spend in interest costs relating to a loan versus what your money could earn if it were to remain invested. For example, if you can borrow money at 3% per annum and your investment is earning 6% per annum, the strategy works. When the cost of borrowing is higher than the earnings that will be created, the strategy doesn't work at all.

Borrowing can be effective where money is invested in growth assets such as shares and property. Shares and property are assets with potential for an increase in value over time, combined with an ability to pay an ongoing income stream—your investment might increase in value as well as providing income. The downside of getting it wrong is that the strategy could end up costing you in losses. Losses can be much bigger than you expect. I always recommend you take professional advice when jumping into a gearing (borrowing) strategy so you truly understand the risks you're about to enter into.

If you are already in debt up to your eyeballs, the best thing you can do is to talk to your credit provider. They have remedies available to assist you, if only you'll pick up the phone and speak to them. Hiding from your creditors only makes things worse.

* * *

Hopefully you now have a handle on the type of debt you have. It's not uncommon to discover most people have a combination of good and bad debt. The trick is to understand what you have and work towards minimising the bad debt you carry.

Let's look at loans in a little more detail, mainly so you understand who benefits when your loan structure is wrong for you. It *is* possible to end up with a loan that suits the lender more than it benefits you.

There are some terms relating to loans you may never have heard of before, but need to know so you understand what the lender is offering.

Another term you're going to hear is 'leverage'. In this case we're not talking about how you might move things about; we're going to consider it in relation to how it helps you achieve your goals.

Mind Your Money Tip

The key to borrowing is discipline.

Chapter 7

Loans and Leverage

'When you combine ignorance and leverage, you get some pretty interesting results.'

—Warren Buffett[13]

Making sure you get the *right type of credit* for you isn't necessarily always easy. While credit providers are willing to extend credit, as borrowers we need to be aware that credit is only ever issued *on the terms of the lender*. As a borrower you don't get a chance to determine the terms of your credit contract; the lender decides the terms and conditions and you have to abide by what they outline.

Before we go any further, let's talk about the difference between a loan and leverage. To the uninitiated, they are the same thing. To those more in the know, there's a huge difference and it's mainly in the definition and the purpose of the borrowing.

According to Investopedia, a loan is 'the act of giving money, property or other material goods to another party in exchange for future repayment of the principal amount along with interest or other finance charges. A loan may be for a specific, one-time amount or can be available as open-ended credit up to a specified ceiling amount'.[14]

---

13 www.brainyquote.com

14 www.investopedia.com/terms/l/loan.asp

Investopedia consider leverage as 'the use of various financial instruments or borrowed capital, such as margin, to increase the potential return of an investment'.[15]

Most typically, leverage is used to complete the purchase of real estate, but it can be used to purchase other investment assets. The funny thing is the average borrower/home owner thinks they've taken out a home loan. They've no idea that they are using leverage (buying an asset they hope goes up in value while they live in it) to complete the transaction.

The right loan for you

It's important to ensure the credit contract you are about to enter is reasonable and acceptable to your personal circumstances.

When a lender offers you a loan, please read the full terms and conditions of the credit contract so you know what you're getting yourself into before you sign on the dotted line.

You should only be prepared to sign contracts and accept the offer *after* you've considered the implications of the terms of credit. A loan contract is not just about how much you have to pay and when. You need to also consider:

* interest rate and monthly fees
* loan term
* security required.

Let's start off with explaining the terms you might come across when you go looking for a loan.

* *Lender or funder*—the provider of your loan. These terms came in after deregulation of banking in Australia as the funder of your loan may not be a bank.
* *Credit provider*—similar in effect to the term of lender or funder; however, it could refer to the provider of your credit

---

15 www.investopedia.com/terms/l/leverage.asp

card, your utilities, a company from which you rent or lease items and maybe even your telecommunications provider. They are considered to be credit providers because they provide you with goods or services on credit.

* *Mortgage*—the document describing the agreement between the lender/funder and the borrower pertaining to the purchase of real property, such as land, a house or other building. A mortgage records the interest (the loan provided) of the lender/funder in the property, which ensures the funder is repaid first in the event of the property being sold.
* *Mortgagor*—the borrower, the person or people responsible for the repayment of the loan.
* *Mortgagee*—the lender/funder with the registered interest in a real property.
* *Charge*—the term used by a credit provider when it's not legally possible to implement a mortgage to acknowledge a debt. A charge is applied to assets purchased using borrowed funds such as motor vehicles, business assets and other items not able to have a registered mortgage taken over them, with the intention of ensuring the credit provider's interest (the loan provided) in the asset is recorded.
* *Guarantor*—someone who agrees to take responsibility for the repayments in case the original borrower doesn't meet their loan repayment obligations. Extreme caution needs to be applied if you are *ever* asked to be a guarantor—more on that later.
* *Guarantee*—the documentation that links a guarantor as being directly responsible for repayment of a loan in the event the original borrower does not repay the debt.
* *Borrower*—the person responsible for any debt repayments relating to a borrowing (loan).

Interest rates and fees

The first thing I encourage clients to do is to check if the interest rate outlined in the loan contract is close to current market rate. What the heck does 'current market rate' mean, and better yet, how do I find that out easily?

You could physically visit a range of banks, but that will take heaps of your time. Or search for rates online by visiting a range of bank websites to compare, but that's time consuming as well but that's time consuming also.

My best suggestion is to get online and start searching for *comparison websites;* it will make your job easy. Comparison sites will have done all the work for you in comparing all factors relating to a proposed loan or other financial products you are considering buying. After a little online homework you will be able to see if the interest rate being offered is close to the current market rate. If it's not, reconsider the offer or you'll pay way more for the item than you had intended.

Let's say you were considering borrowing $5000 for furniture with a loan term of three years. Let's look at the impact of getting the wrong interest rate.

Amount borrowed: $5000 Loan term: 3 years

	Credit provider A	**Credit provider B**	**Credit provider C**
Interest	7.95%pa + $10 pm fee	13.95% pa+ $10 pm fee	21.95%pa+ $10 pm fee
Monthly payment	$167 per month	$181 per month	$201 per month
Total payment	$6012	$6516	$7236

Credit provider A gets my vote. Interest rates and monthly fees are important considerations. The moral of the story is to check the details of your credit contract! If you don't understand the contract, get financial or legal advice.

Loan term

If you're thinking about taking a loan over a longer term to make the repayments more affordable, you will end up paying more than you would have if you had elected to take the loan over a shorter term.

Using the same loan contracts we considered previously, let's increase the loan term from three years to five years. *Note the difference in the total amount you pay over the whole term of the loan.*

Amount borrowed: $5000 Loan term: 5 years

	Credit provider A	Credit provider B	Credit provider C
Interest	7.95%pa + $10 pm fee	13.95% pa+ $10 pm fee	21.95%pa+ $10 pm fee
Monthly payment	$167 per month	$126 per month	$148 per month
Total payment	$6660	$7560	$8880

As you can see in the table above, by reducing your monthly repayment and lengthening the loan term, that $5000 worth of furniture can end up costing anywhere between $6660 and $8880. That's right; you end up paying an extra $2220 for the same furniture.

Security

Have you ever wondered what 'security' means when you hear people talking about borrowing? Security is the asset the lender wants to take a mortgage or a charge over. If we think about your home, the lender/ bank effectively owns your home.

The most common example of a lender taking security over an asset is when you buy a property and the lender takes a mortgage over the property as a condition of funding the loan. If you don't make the repayments, the lender/bank can repossess the asset to recover any money they consider you owe them. When people don't stay within the terms of a loan agreement, the lender has the right to recoup their money by selling the property.

Unsecured loans

If the lender decides not to, or is unable to take security for a loan, they will offer an unsecured loan. As the lender isn't going to have an asset to sell should you default on your loan agreement, they will take other actions to offset the additional risk they are taking in lending you the money. This may sound like gobbledygook. Let me explain.

The lender considers ways they can recoup losses if you decide not to make your loan repayments. The lender expects borrowers to *pay a penalty* for not providing them with security. The penalty will be in the form of you paying *a higher interest rate for the duration of the loan term*.

Depending on the lender and the borrower's credit history, the 'penalty' interest rate you will pay for not providing security for your borrowing can be anything from 2–3 % per annum right through to in excess of 10% per annum. Electing not to provide security can cost you dearly and will hurt your hip pocket.

* * *

As you can see, just those three factors—interest rate, term and security—can make a huge difference to the outcome of your loan experience. The choice of loan contract determines the amount of money you truly end up paying for the items you've elected to buy.

It's crazy to spend more than you need to just to provide the lender with a bigger profit. *Be sure your loan contract gives you the best outcome, not the lender.*

The cost of apathy

Do you suffer from procrastination? You aren't on your own. Have you ever stopped to consider the cost of that single delaying tactic? It's quite likely to be costing you a bucket load of cash each and every year. How so?

Is there a credit card loan that you can't manage to pay off in full each month? It's costing you money for each day that you don't get around to paying it off or refinancing your debt to a lower interest rate account (more on refinancing later).

Most people who don't pay off their credit card have a balance of around $10 000 outstanding on their account. If your credit card has an interest rate of 18.95% per annum and you pay the minimum payment of $204 in the first month, according to the Money Smart website you can expect to pay back $39 288 over 47 years and two months.[16]

Outstanding credit card debt $10 000

Interest Rate	Minimum Repayment	Repayment Term	Total Repayment
18.95%p.a.	$204	47 years 2 months	$39 288

However, if time is taken to refinance that account to a lower rate credit card account you will save yourself a considerable sum. If you have the same initial loan, but the interest rate is reduced to 11.95% per annum and you still only pay the minimum payment of $202 in the first month, according to the Money Smart website you can expect to pay back $19 142 over 24 years and six months.

You will achieve even better results if you elect to pay higher repayments. The table below shows the impact of refinancing and paying more:

16 www.moneysmart.gov.au/tools-and-resources/calculators-and-tools/credit-card-calculator

Interest Rate	18.95% pa	11.95% pa
Minimum Repayment	$204	$202
Original Repayment Term	47 years 2 months	24 years 6 months
Total Repayment	$39 288	$19 142
Increased Repayment	$476	$476
NEW Repayment Term	2 years	2 years
Total Repayment	$11 181	$11 181
Potential Savings	$28 107	$7961

Another way to reduce the term and total cost of the loan easily would be to make more frequent repayments than outlined in the contract.

Weekly repayments instead of monthly repayments can add up to a huge saving.

What if I'm struggling?

You've probably managed to rack up quite a few loans and credit facilities since you started working.

Have you got so many loans you really don't know how you're going to repay them all? Rather than going into a panic or putting your head in the sand, let us consider options that may get you out of a bind.

Because you've decided it's time to take back control of your finances, where to from now? Try not to get behind in paying your loan repayments otherwise your credit rating will be affected. Let's look at:

* not ignoring creditors
* refinancing high interest loans to low interest
* credit balance transfers
* restructuring your loan
* paying off the highest interest loan first.

Talk to creditors

We're only going to touch briefly on the importance of communicating with your creditors in this section. Have you ever heard that old saying, 'Prevention is better than cure?' The same thing applies to your credit history and how you manage your obligations; it's best not to make mistakes.

Do *not* put your head in the sand. *Not opening your mail* so you can ignore bills is asking for trouble. Start talking to creditors.

Many people think a credit provider and a debt collector are the same. They're very different. A credit provider is a company; probably a lender, utilities or telecommunications provider that provided you with products or services and you owe them money for what they've supplied.

A debt collector is a person or company responsible for recovering any money you owe the credit provider. Some credit providers may sell your debt (the amount you owe them) to a debt collector, who will then step up activities to recover the money you *now* owe the debt collection company.

If you aren't paying bills on time and in full, *contact the credit provider and explain your changed circumstances*. It's much better to talk to your creditors than it is to hide from them. Communication is a key to getting out of a financial pickle, particularly if there are no alternatives.

To encourage them to assist you, share:

* if the issue is temporary or long term (e.g. you've lost your job)
* options you propose for repayment (how much and how frequently).

Information is incredibly important in helping them decide whether they are willing to work with you to protect your credit rating or not. Companies often have internal recovery teams that will work with you to recover the money owed. They have the power to help you reach payment terms and stop interest accruing. They can even stop late fees being applied—*but only if you talk to them.*

Communicating might stop escalation of recovery efforts and stop them from referring the matter to a debt collector.

Debt collectors want to be paid and often don't care about damaging your credit rating. Do what you can to avoid getting referred to a debt collection agency because by the time a matter is referred to debt collection, your credit history (credit rating) has likely already been badly damaged.

Your credit rating is your personal financial reputation. We look after our reputations; we *need* to look after our credit rating too. We'll talk some more about protecting your credit rating in *Part 3 Protect Yourself*, as there are many other scenarios where inaction can impact your credit rating.

Communicate. Collections people can't help unless you ask. Swallow that pride for a second and start taking or returning calls before things get out of hand.

Refinancing

Getting more credit? If I'm struggling and trying to pay off my loans, why go get more credit? Really?

Yes, but with qualifications, and *only* if it's viable to reduce the ongoing costs of existing debts. Getting more credit is not a workable suitable solution if you are *adding* to existing debt levels. However, refinancing debts can be a suitable solution when you are refinancing your high interest rate loans, such as credit cards, into a lower cost loan facility. There is a big *but* …

Refinancing your debts into a lower cost loan is only an acceptable option if you *cut up the credit cards and totally cancel the credit card facility.*

Refinancing loans in this instance focuses on reducing the cost of managing your repayment obligations so you pay less in the long run. It's completely different to 'consolidating' your loans. We'll look at that a little later.

I've put together a scenario that is all too familiar in these days of easy credit for us to consider. Let's pretend the loans are yours.

There's a total of $79 000 owing—three credit cards and two loans—with no real assets to show for all that spending. Assets are saleable items. (Refer to table on page 110 and 111.)

Your car cost $29 000 your car loan is $27 000. You have $2000 in equity in the car.

Approach a credit provider to refinance your debts; it's a great starting point. Refinancing can only happen if a credit provider is willing to bundle up what you owe other lenders into a single loan. Effectively, they agree to offer a loan that will allow your other loan obligations to be repaid; you make a single payment to one place instead of two or three. Be aware, not all credit providers are keen on refinancing past a certain amount (the amount depends on the credit provider) *unless* there is security available. It's understandable really; they're taking on a *much* bigger risk.

The aim of the game is to refinance the debts to lower interest rates that you're paying now. Once you refinance it's important to:

- remove the temptation of credit card spending by cancelling the accounts and cutting up the cards
- make the same repayment amount you did previously, it's a great way to take advantage of the reduction in interest charges. The debt should take less time to repay and cost less in the long run.

Researching refinance options on comparison websites is a great place to start; you can compare options suitable to your needs.

Each provider/funder has specific requirements you have to meet if they are going to be willing to refinance your debts from another provider. You should know, if you go to your bank to refinance what you owe them, there's a pretty strong chance the answer will be 'no'—go to another credit provider instead.

Unless you are planning on borrowing more from a credit provider, there's no advantage to them in offering you a better deal. It sounds tough, but what we as consumers need to understand is that credit providers aren't in business to do us favours. They're in business to make profits.

Loans	**Personal Loan**	**Car Loan**
Amount owing	$12 000	$27 000
Purpose	Holiday (two years ago)	Car
Interest rate pa	13.90%	5.00%
Ongoing annual fees	$72	$0
Annual interest cost (simple interest)	$1668	$1350
Minimum monthly payment	$327	$522
Remaining loan term	24 months	48 months

CREDIT CARDS	Card 1	Card 2	Card 3
Amount owing	$20 000	$15 000	$5000
Purpose	Spending habits	Spending habits	Furniture purchase
Interest rate pa	20.00%	13.50%	30.00%
Ongoing annual fees	$150	$70	$60
Annual interest cost (simple interest)	$4000	$2025	$0*
Minimum % payment	2.00	2.00	0.00
Minimum monthly payment	$400	$300	$0
Interest fee period	N/A	N/A	36 months
Interest free period ends	N/A	N/A	24 months

*currently in an interest free period

Transfer

Credit providers love the chance to transfer the balance outstanding on your existing credit card to them. Most providers only offer balance transfer specials a few times a year; you can't expect to access a balance transfer deal all year round.

No single credit card provider specialises in balance transfer offers; they all offer special rates when it suits them. If a credit card provider does have a permanent balance transfer offer, it's usually at a much higher interest rate than the rate that's on offer when special offers available.

Balance transfer providers offer enticing interest rates, anywhere between 0–6% for introductory periods, usually between 6–18 months. After the introductory period ends, borrowers pay the interest rate applicable to that card. Again, refer to the comparison websites to check your options. Often, advertised rates end up having hidden traps like high annual fees or higher interest rates at the end of the special offer period.

For the disciplined, balance transfers can allow you to seriously focus on paying down debt. For the less disciplined, a balance transfer can simply delay the inevitable. There will be a period where only the minimum repayment is made, until finally the higher interest rate kicks in and debt gets out of hand again.

If you use a balance transfer offer, the key is not to spend more—cut up the card that comes with the offer of finance so you can't be tempted to spend more.

Take advantage of the strategy by paying significantly more than the minimum payment each month. Ideally, work out what it will take to pay the whole debt off within the introductory interest rate period. If you aren't able to pay the amount off in full during the introductory interest rate period, pay as much as you can each month to reduce the overall amount you owe.

Restructuring

Did you know you can refinance your credit card debt with a structured loan, with a set term, fixed interest rate and repayment amounts? Most people aren't aware restructuring a loan can create an advantage by reducing the ongoing cost of the loan and paying it off as quickly as possible.

A loan with a structure is referred to as a term loan—it has a set term, interest rate and repayment schedule. It will fully repay the original borrowed amount and interest charges over the stated period; think home loan, personal loan or car loan.

The personal and car loans in our scenario are examples of structured term loans. Unfortunately, credit cards are not term loans—they do not have a structure that creates discipline which will result in the debt being repaid. Credit card providers consider that providing you make the minimum repayment each month and are within your agreed limit, you are within the terms of the agreement.

A credit card has no requirement to repay the outstanding amount. Credit providers prefer it when you don't; they charge interest every time you don't repay your debt in full. Credit card providers frequently reward people with offers to increase the credit available. Offers are *not* made because the credit provider likes you. If you take up the offer, their profits will increase at *your* expense.

Why a loan with a structured term and repayments, not a credit card? Because a term loan is designed be repaid and can help to reign in unwieldy credit card debt.

A credit provider is legally required to make you an offer of finance by issuing a contract that outlines:

* the interest rate
* how much interest it will cost you if you make all of your repayments on time (total borrowings)
* monthly payment (loan repayments)
* the loan term (how many loan repayments you are required to make)
* penalties that may apply if you don't meet the loan terms outlined in the credit contract. This is usually a higher interest rate but can also include late and penalty fees.

Repayment makeover

There are ways to reduce the amount of interest you pay and speed up how long it takes to repay your loan. You could:

* focus on repaying extra on the highest interest rate loan first
* pay more than the minimum payment each month
* increase how often you repay your loan
* pay off debts with interest-free periods within the interest free period.

Be sure not to ignore one loan or to favour one provider over another. Pay everyone on time the full amount of the due repayment.

If you have extra cash, it can be helpful if you start by applying the extra cash to *repaying the highest interest rate first.*

By electing to *pay more than the minimum payment each month* you will save interest charges. If you pay off the highest interest rate loan first, you still have to meet your obligations in relation to *all* of your credit and loan obligations. You'd be surprised what a difference paying an additional $10 or $20 per repayment can make to the term of your loan. You could save months or even years off your loan term. Jump onto your bank's website and have a little play around with their free calculators and see how much you can save. They show in real terms how much interest and how many months or years' worth of repayments you won't have to make.

A really effective move is to *increase the frequency by which you repay your loan.* A loan contract requires monthly repayments, yet switching up the frequency of payments can make a huge impact to the amount of interest you will pay. Pay the equivalent of required monthly repayments, but make your payments each week instead of monthly.

I've been using this strategy forever—well before banks made it public it was possible to make repayments to your home loan more frequently than monthly. A friend recently discovered the power of the strategy accidentally when trying to figure out what she could afford to borrow to buy a new home. She was absolutely horrified by how much money she 'wasted' by not paying her home loan on a weekly basis. She was so ticked off it reminded me to share this simple strategy so you save too.

The strategy works on any loan. Simply divide the monthly repayment by four and start making weekly payments. You reduce the amount of interest charged to your loans and you will make the equivalent of 13 monthly payments in a year rather than the required 12. You will repay your loan earlier than expected and you will save significant amounts in interest charges too.

In our scenario, Card 3 has 24 months remaining on the interest-free period. I encourage you to *focus on the amount you need to save in order to pay your debt off by the end of the interest-free period.*

This will be your most expensive credit facility if you don't pay it off during the interest-free period. If you haven't paid it off in full by the expiry of the interest-free period, the credit provider has the right to go right back to day one of the credit contract and to start charging you interest on the full amount from that day. You need to be aware of the sting in the tail of this credit contract.

If you calculate the required amount to clear Card 3 to be $5180 (the current debt plus three times the annual fee), you will have to save $216 per month towards paying it. Be smart; save the funds before the end of the interest-free period, so you are in a position to repay the loan in full. If you can't trust yourself to save the money, pay amounts to the loan each week or month; it achieves the same result.

* * *

We've touched on the how and why of paying off loans that were primarily for personal use, yet sometimes borrowings are for investment purposes. Let's consider why people use leverage to purchase assets, assets with potential to either increase in value or to pay an income, and how you can use it to your advantage. Leverage is really just another name for borrowing, although it's generally a term used when there's an intention to create wealth behind the borrowing.

Leverage—good, bad and ugly

Leverage happens when you borrow money to buy an asset. When we buy an asset and can't use cash to pay in full for the item, we use leverage. An asset purchased with the intention of making a profit, using borrowed money, can be considered to be using leverage to your advantage.

In Australia, leverage is most frequently used to buy property investments, including the family home, with the property expected to provide capital appreciation (an increase in the value of an asset when compared to the price paid for it) and rental income, if the property is being leased to tenants.

Leverage can be used to buy other assets such as shares and managed fund portfolios too. Again, these investment assets are expected to increase in capital value and to provide income by way of dividends to shareholders. Share dividends generally come from company profits, with each shareholder being entitled to a share of company profits depending on their shareholding.

Leverage can be a powerful tool, yet it comes with inherent risks that aren't evident when markets (both property and share markets) are rising. As markets rise, returns are magnified because investor profits cover (or mask) the cost of borrowing.

I've never heard anyone complain about leverage when the markets are going up. The same can't be said when the markets are going down though. Complaints about losses are long and loud.

As the property market goes up, people are happy; it means they have more equity in their home. When the market goes down, it can get to a point where the debt is more than the property would be worth if the property were sold. In downward trending markets there is not much evidence of excited vendors, because they stand to make a loss or only end up with a small profit after the loans are repaid.

When investment markets are falling, the power of leverage can come back to bite an unsuspecting borrower. Depending on how aggressively you've used leverage, sometimes the bite can be savage! Let me explain.

Using borrowed money to invest, you have more money in the market. If the market goes down, your losses will be magnified. You stand to lose far more using borrowed money than you would if you had only used your own money. How can you lose more money when you've used borrowed money to invest? To be honest, it's got nothing to do with the size of your loan; it's got everything to do with the changing value of what you invested in. I have discussed buying shares at bargain basement prices and making a profit, yet it's important to realise you won't always make a profit when buying investments. The table below goes a long way to explaining why you stand to lose much more when you borrow money to invest when compared to using only your own money

	Using my own money	**Using my own money and equal amount of borrowed funds**
Share price at time of purchase	$35.00	$35.00
Number purchased	285	571
Initial portfolio value	$10 000	$20 000
Current share price	$15.30	$15.30
New market value	$4360.50	$8736.30
Potential loss	$5639.50	$11 263.70

Many things should influence a decision to use leverage to achieve your goal or not. 'If you're prepared to use it (leverage), be prepared to lose it (your money and possibly more)', has always been my motto when it comes to leverage.

Individuals tend to think we have 'things' under control; however, unexpected impacts like market forces, interest rate changes and economic cycles have significant impacts on the decision to use leverage or not.

Risk management must play a very significant role in your decision to use leverage. You need cash reserves and exit strategies planned. Leaving such important factors to luck could cause a very expensive mistake.

During the Global Financial Crisis (GFC), I worked in a practice which concentrated on double gearing strategies. According to the practice owner, it was a foolproof way to make money—there is *no* foolproof way to make money.

Clients thought he was a genius, simply because the market was booming and results were exceptional. While markets were booming, he and many others were busy ignoring the potential downside risks.

Use of a double gearing strategy can be extremely risky. Full of rewards when markets are rising and potentially devastating when it goes wrong, as it did in the GFC.

I remember meeting with a couple mid-GFC; the value of their investments had more than halved. Associated debt was $100 000 and their investment was around $48 000. Their initial investment had been started with borrowed money.

Sally was the deputy principal of a local school, usually so assured and very proper. Tears streamed down her face; she was emotionally devastated. In her mind's eye she saw everything they had worked for crumbling and disappearing before her eyes. She visualised the loss of their home, her husband's business—their security. It terrified her.

She sobbed, 'I can't take this anymore. Sell the lot'. With some reassurance, lots of hand holding plus some effective re-planning, they didn't need to sell. This turned out to be a great outcome; the apparent losses stayed on paper rather than being turned into actual losses as would have happened if the assets had been sold. Given time, the value of their investments recovered almost to the starting point. She shed tears and did lose sleep; yet all the things she had visualised didn't actually occur.

The financial fallout for them, if they hadn't held the strategy, could've been devastating. Had they sold the portfolio, they would have lost money by selling for *much* less than the assets had cost them, but they would still have to repay the debt. By retaining the strategy, the portfolio had time to recover in value *and* to pay income to assist with the cost of the loans. Investment related loans provided tax advantages, which assisted with cash flow. It wasn't a perfect solution, yet it was a much better outcome than it could have been had they acted and sold it all.

This is an example of *Bad and Ugly Leverage*; the clients truly didn't understand the risks they were taking. If the loans had been incorrectly structured, their home could have been at risk; correct structuring meant their home was safe. Too high an appetite for risk combined with greed and poor planning can be a fatal combination when it comes to people's finances.

Effective leverage

Leverage, even allowing for associated risks, can be an incredibly powerful tool that provides positive results when used effectively.

During the GFC, long-term share investors better understood the risks they were taking. The degree of risk was acceptable because in previous years they had benefited from annual returns in excess of 30% per annum for multiple years in a row.

The gains (increases in value) within their portfolios meant they were better insulated from the risk of having to sell all or part of their portfolios at a loss. Using the double leverage strategy, these clients had successfully paid off their personal mortgages and only had tax-effective, investment-related debt remaining. Changes in value remained on paper, simply because they were able to preserve the value of portfolios.

A decision to leverage the purchase of any asset comes with both positive and negative attributes that need to be planned for. Be aware and know the risks before you face them. Keep cash reserves available and have an exit plan in case things go wrong. Do not leave it to luck. Plan, plan, plan!

Mind Your Money Tip

Use leverage judiciously. Weigh up the potential rewards as well as the risks. Have an exit strategy, even if it means selling at a loss.

Part 3

PROTECT YOURSELF!

Chapter 8

Your Credit Rating

'Remember that credit is money.'

—Benjamin Franklin

Have you ever heard someone complain they can't get a loan because of a poor credit history? A whole section of the finance industry focuses on people with poor credit histories, which means having a poor or impaired credit history is not uncommon. Having an impaired credit history is a nice way of saying 'bad payers'. Bad payers are penalised in future credit dealings—that's assuming they are actually able to get additional credit.

Protecting your credit rating might sound crazy; however, it is vitally important to the way you access credit in the future. If you're an adult who has a telephone service or sought credit, you have a credit history.

There *is* a difference between your credit history and your credit rating from a credit provider's perspective. A credit history shows the credit for which you've applied. Those silly little bills you forgot to pay are recorded. Credit applications are reported, even if you decide not to take the loan, to a central credit reporting agency, currently Veda Advantage in Australia.

Credit ratings tell the story of past and current management of existing credit facilities, including loans; key ingredients used by potential credit providers to assess a credit application. They consider the current conduct of loans—credit facilities (phone, electricity, video store etc.) and decide whether to grant a new loan after considering what's recorded on your credit report.

I said to be nice to recovery people and debt collectors—this is why they're interrelated. It could be what saves your credit report from a negative notation. It's up to the discretion of the debt collector whether they note your credit history or not. If you communicate with creditors, and they believe you are acting in good faith, there is less likelihood of information that may damage your credit rating being reported.

If you're like most people, you may have managed to accumulate quite a bit of debt and accessed quite a bit of credit since you started working. You haven't missed a payment, but can you say all the repayments were on time? Late payments come with more than a late fee. Now late payments can be recorded on your credit history.

Avoid being reported

Be very, very careful…

Legislative changes mean scheduled payments, including loan repayments made more than five days late, can result in credit providers adding notations about defaults to your credit report. The industry treats such notations as 'black marks'. An accumulation of black marks will directly impact your ability to access additional credit.

It's really important to be aware if something is recorded against your credit history; the impact is for many years, not just a few days. Recently I saw a TV ad focused on providing loans to people with bad credit histories. The credit provider offered to ignore poor credit history reports and to extend even more credit.

Be careful of taking on more credit if you have already been struggling with your existing loans and a poor credit history. The promise to ignore previous poor credit history comes with a cost. A credit impaired borrower, industry speak for bad payers, pays much higher interest charges to cover the additional risk the lender knows they are taking. Interestingly, research revealed a surprisingly simple reason for people's credit histories being impacted: moving house and not providing a new address to the credit provider.

Who knew it could be that simple?

A young woman I know moved out of a shared flat, assuming her mail would be forwarded—it wasn't. An electricity provider recorded a default because of an unpaid electricity bill. She 'discovered' the unpaid bill when she tried to finance a car. She couldn't get finance until she could prove she had paid the electricity bill.

Do what you can to protect your credit history; it's protecting your money reputation.

Credit isn't just loans

When we 'open' an account with a provider—think phone, internet and electricity—we are effectively entering into an credit contract. We have asked the provider to *extend us credit* when we buy their services.

There's another very important type of credit most people don't consider—a rental agreement or a lease. Having been both a tenant and a landlord, I understand the importance of making payments on time from both sides of the equation. When a tenant misses paying rent, pays late or falls behind, it's the responsibility of the property manager to turn debt collector.

Falling behind in rent payments is reported to a central tenancy agency. Not paying, or paying late, can result in you being put on a 'tenancy black list'.

Future property managers and landlords will use the register to assess whether you should be granted a lease. Being reported reduces the chances of getting future rental properties. Once a tenant is evicted it's almost impossible for them to access quality housing in the future.

People tend to overlook late fees at the video store. Putting your head in the sand and ignoring a small amount can be a *big* mistake in the making! Store owners habitually report small debts. One store owner had no idea of the implications herself until someone did it to her. She went white when she discovered she couldn't get a home loan because of numerous reports from video stores on her credit report. Only when it was too late did she understand the impact.

It's time to stop haphazardly paying your bills and be focused; pay on time and in full. It takes many years to 'correct' a poor credit history. In the eyes of the credit providers a poor history *never* really goes away.

Beware of phone contracts

I had a dispute with a phone provider in 2011. I entered into a phone contract without knowing my home was in a known black spot for the carrier. My mobile phone was as useful as a paperweight when it came to making or taking calls. Given that I run my business from a home office, it was a disaster.

After many complaints and the intervention of the Telecommunications Ombudsman, I was released from the contract, without penalty, on the proviso I returned the handset. Easy! The handset was returned in a satchel provided by them so it could be tracked within their billing system. The handset was returned yet I kept getting big bills. What a mix up!

Six months of calling the billing section of the company achieved nothing. They kept sending letters of demand. I was becoming concerned for my personal credit history. *I recorded the name, time and date of each contact.* This was a huge advantage to backing up my claims regarding the terms of cancelling the contract. Finally, a letter arrived threatening to list defaults on public records—I was not a happy camper!

The irony of the situation was the whole chaotic scenario was a result of inefficiencies within the company; nothing was my fault.

Do all you can to protect your credit rating.

When it comes to credit 'Big Brother' watches and records everything. Try not to over-commit yourself. If you can't afford something, don't take it on. Maybe consider pre-paid options, because then you truly can decide how and when you spend your money

You may have thought protecting your credit rating meant very little until now. To a credit provider it's one of the first measures they look at when deciding to lend you money or not. Even though your credit rating isn't of much interest to you, you can rest assured it makes interesting reading to future credit providers.

Mind Your Money Tip

Look after your credit rating—it's your money reputation!

Chapter 9

Relationship STDs

'This would be a much better world if more married couples were as deeply in love as they are in debt.'

—Earl Wilson[17]

What have STDs got to do with money? It's not what you are thinking! We are talking Sexually Transmitted Debts. STDs can be highly contagious and financially debilitating, with long lasting symptoms and unwanted side effects.

Are you in a serious relationship? Then this section is a must for you. Let's make sure you are financially protected, so you don't end up with unwanted debts from being in a relationship with a financially irresponsible person.

There's an old Meatloaf song, '*I would do anything for love*'. Would you? Many will say 'yes'. Yet acting through the blinkers of love has potential to damage your financial health if something goes wrong with the relationship.

Trusting partners, fully equipped with rose-coloured glasses, assume their relationship will last. Yet being in a relationship is not a protection for our assets; it's more of a risk. Often being in a relationship, or helping family out, can be the very reason you lose your assets.

---

17 http://www.brainyquote.com/quotes/quotes/e/earlwilson386861.html?src=t_debt

STDs—highly contagious!

Think of the relationships you know where one party has way more to bring to the arrangement than the other party. Often the other partner comes with more debt and limited assets—there really isn't a balance.

The story of 'Jane and her STD' sadly is typical. Jane was a smart cookie; she bought a house and had been actively paying it off. Her home was worth $500 000 and through consistent diligent management of her expenses she only had $200 000 left on her mortgage.

Her squeeze, Tarzan, had lived a liberal life—lots of fun and overseas travel. He brought a stack of debt and his car to the relationship: three credit cards totalling $70 000 and a car loan of $25 000. Not a lot to show financially, but he'd had a really good time.

Jane and Tarzan decided to move in together and made plans for a combined future. Jane worried about the interest Tarzan was paying on his credit card debts. She knew credit card interest was at least 20% per annum. The car loan was costing Tarzan 10% per annum and Jane couldn't see a way for Tarzan to pay off his debts quickly if his loans stayed the same. Jane knew her home loan interest rate was only costing her about 5.5% per annum.

Being in what she considered a committed relationship, Jane offered to speak to her bank about refinancing his debts. The plan was to use her home as collateral for his loans, so Tarzan could take advantage of much lower home loan interest rates. Jane was aware of the potential to save them heaps if the loans were refinanced using her home as collateral.

If the bank agreed to refinance Tarzan's loans the total mortgage against Jane's property would increase by $95 000. Tarzan's unsecured loans would be cleared using a secured loan against Jane's property, secured by way of a personal guarantee from Jane. *Of course*, he would be responsible for loan repayments; it was the least he could do.

The bank didn't have a problem with the refinance using Jane's collateral. Usually, banks will grant a loan happily if collateral is available and there is an apparent way of repaying a loan. There was never really a barrier to refinancing Tarzan's loan; Jane had plenty of equity available in her property and they both had jobs. The bank wanted a guarantee from Jane before completing Tarzan's loan, telling Jane a guarantee was simply a formality.

Tarzan thought of the money he could save. Jane saw nothing wrong with it either. As a couple, they would both benefit from the savings.

Around three months later they started fighting; he'd been cheating on her. She was devastated and kicked him out. Locks were changed; she was determined he wasn't coming back. The cheating swine!

Jane's STD infection started to raise its head. She had been blissfully unaware of the festering infection that started when she allowed Tarzan to refinance his loans. Once Tarzan was kicked out, the STD infection got out of control because Tarzan refused to repay his loan.

Because Jane had guaranteed the loan, the bank approached Jane to start paying Tarzan's loan. By guaranteeing Tarzan's loan, an unsuspecting Jane effectively had agreed to repay his debts if he couldn't or wouldn't. She'd had *no idea of what she'd agreed to* until it was way too late!

The bank reminded Jane the loan was secured by way of a mortgage against her home. Should she decide not to repay Tarzan's loan, the bank would have the legal right to sell her home to recover the outstanding monies. She was stunned!

She sought legal advice, only to have it confirmed—if she wanted to keep the roof over her head, she would be forced not only to repay her own mortgage, she also had to take responsibility for repaying Tarzan's loan.

Jane realised she would have been much smarter to have assisted him:

* to refinance his credit card debt to a lower interest rate debt, where he remained responsible for his debts or
* by helping him pay off his existing loans if he couldn't refinance them on his own.

Had she done either of the above, Tarzan's debt would still be his. Jane's home would be safe, not at risk as a result of a poorly conceived debt restructure.

STDs can and do impact the financial health of both sexes. STDs are transmitted between those with assets and those with debts, usually while the parties are in a state of euphoria, induced by love.

A word to the wise: Borrowing against the other person's assets can have consequences! You could be paying the price of an STD infection for many years to come—as many years as it takes to pay off the loan.

Joint arrangements

Joint financial arrangements sound fine and rosy, a commitment even. I remember those heady stages and thinking the easiest solution was to pool our finances. I was the doer, responsible for paying bills and arranging things; a joint account would make my life a heck of a lot easier, I thought. I remember a dispute over the trust required to join our finances. My attitude was: If you can't trust me, don't bother to marry me. In hindsight, this was quite a big statement from a 19-year-old!

Since then, many times I've wished we'd retained individual personal accounts and agreed to create a joint account through which to manage joint obligations. Everything has been going into the same joint melting pot for years because of my early insistence.

I no longer advocate for a total melding of financial resources. This change of attitude has occurred for a number of very valid reasons that have nothing to do with my personal situation. There are some very powerful reasons for you to *consider having a filter between your personal finances and those you hold jointly with your partner*. Let's consider a few reasons why you need to protect your *ass-ets* (your butt and your assets) with the correct ownership structures.

Unintended side effects

Joint assets are not just bank accounts; it's more far reaching that that.

In Australia we generally buy assets as joint tenants without really knowing what that means legally. Assets owned by more than a single person causes joint ownership; everything from bank accounts to managed funds and share portfolios and even property can be jointly owned.

Buying assets as a joint tenant is often an automatic 'choice' over which you have no direct control; think bank accounts, managed funds and shares—you have no alternative.

Therefore, in the event of a single joint owner dying, the surviving person receives the dead person's share of the jointly owned asset. This is known as survivorship.

Where's the problem? The deceased person may have intended their 'share' of the asset to go to someone else entirely!

With property it can be different; it's possible to decide who owns how much of a property in percentage terms. If you don't speak up, the asset will automatically be purchased as joint tenants.

While it is legally possible to stipulate who owns what percentage of a property asset, this creates a 'tenants in common' situation, which comes with some serious advantages if you need to control who gets what from your estate. Nominating percentages of ownership generally is done before the asset is purchased, although it can be adjusted later if you decide it's appropriate to make changes. Owning property as tenants in common, rather than as joint tenants, means you can decide to whom to bequeath your portion of the asset.

As a joint tenant, you might inherit the other half of the joint asset; you also inherit the dead person's share of loans when you have borrowed jointly. As joint borrowers, a bank will hold the survivor liable for the entire debt.

Buying assets as joint tenants can create repercussions you may not even have considered. Let's consider a few scenarios.

Disinheriting your children

If you are part of a blended family this is important to you.

You've each made financial contributions to buying a new home; you want to make provisions for the survivor to stay in the home should you pass away. You've spoken to your newly blended family about the importance of providing support to each other as you age. You want to make sure your own children get their share of the assets you brought to your new relationship.

One of you passes away, and as joint tenants the survivor inherits the home. The person who died first just disinherited their children, simply by dying first.

The entire value of the property transfers to the survivor. The survivor controls who their estate will be distributed to; their own children will be favoured over the children of their deceased partner. In fact, there is no legal need for the children of the deceased partner to be mentioned in the will of the survivor.

Accidentally disinheriting the children of the person who passed could have been avoided if the property had been purchased as tenants in common.

Business failure

Business failure and loss of assets are common. Poor business practices or a personal bankruptcy can result in the loss of assets.

Most credit providers require security before they will extend large amounts of credit, particularly when one person is self-employed. The most significant asset is the family home and without understanding the implications, the business owner and their partner allow the credit provider to take a mortgage over the family home.

If you aren't paying, the mortgagor (the lender) now has the right to force you to sell your family home and whatever else you've promised them (this could be multiple properties) to repay your debts. You may or may not be left with money after your loans are paid out; it all depends on how aggressive the lender is in selling your assets from under you.

Guarantees—the hidden sting

A personal or director's guarantee has much the same impact, although at times it can be far worse for an unsuspecting guarantor. Most guarantors don't fully understand the implications of what they are being asked to do; effectively they guarantee to repay the debt of the person for whom they are providing the guarantee.

A lender/bank requests a personal or director's guarantee, to add an extra layer of protection for them. When the lender considers there is a bigger risk of the venture failing, they want someone else to 'go after' to get their money if their suspicions are proved correct.

Credit providers don't care if you, the guarantor, will be able to repay the debt from personal income, savings or the forced sale of assets. They care about getting their money back if the original borrower defaults on the loan arrangements.

Bad habits

Personal habits can wreak havoc on finances and result in significant financial pain and losses.

A long-term family friend has a serious gambling habit. Money meant to pay wages, bills and to put food on the table is gambled. Poker machines fed her all-encompassing gambling addiction. Never does she tell the true cost of the losses required for each of her 'wins'.

Her habit is so destructive; they have been forced into bankruptcy. Her husband works for someone else and provides her an allowance. It's the only way they can to manage to pay bills and to keep a roof over their heads.

Being too trusting

Trusting too much can get you into lots of trouble financially.

Our friend, whose business had been successfully making ever increasing profits for over 25 years, suddenly found the business was no longer profitable. Neither he nor his business partner could figure out what was suddenly going wrong; they were doing nothing different from their proven formula for success.

Their health suffered. They couldn't work out why sales were up, yet there was no money in the bank and the tax office were asking for payment. They were facing serious financial trouble for the first time ever.

An employee called in sick, so our friend totalled the day's sales. They'd had a tremendous day. It got him thinking and investigating—something was wrong with the books.

The core of their woes was trust; they believed everyone could be trusted. They'd trusted the very person ripping them off. The woman was arrested and business problems solved. The cost of their trust could be measured, more than $300 000 taken over six months.

Each of the business partners had guaranteed the business using their homes; both were at risk of losing their homes had they not solved their business problem.

Domestic violence

Domestic violence and abuse is often an unspoken crime, inflicted by those who are meant to be trustworthy, against those who trust. Some abuse can have no notable physical signs of damage; it can be verbal, emotional, psychological, sexual and financial. The damage is internalised and hidden from public view.

Abuse leaves victims vulnerable; in fear for their safety, usually with no resources available to escape the situation. In many instances the self-esteem of the victim has been seriously damaged. They don't believe they are worthy of help. They are often brainwashed into believing they are worthless; unable to manage without the financial and emotional support of the abuser.

A financial escape route might just provide reassurance and potential freedom to the abused. I now believe each member of a couple should have an emergency fund, something the other party has no control over. The amount is entirely up to you.

New financial territory

You've got a few miles on the clock and you're still recovering from the emotional and financial fallout from your last relationship. The relationship was over ages ago and yet you're still paying the price.

You're never going to leave yourself financially vulnerable again. Yet you are now embarking on a new relationship.

From an emotional viewpoint there's not a lot you can do because right now you're in the early stages of lust and a new relationship! While others could be thinking, *This woman is crazy!* you feel your relationship is strong and this one won't go pear shaped. You both trust each other to be fair and think you don't need a financial agreement.

It is normal and healthy at the beginning of a relationship to think that it is strong . But it's worth knowing there are steps you can take to protect yourself and your assets. I've outlined some risks below. Be sure to discuss it with your legal adviser. This is my understanding and is not legal advice.

Co-habitation agreements

Most of you are likely to be blissfully unaware of the financial risks of entering a relationship, particularly if there is a financial imbalance. You assume it will be necessary to fight out a settlement if the relationship crashes and burns.

A solicitor friend was telling me why everyone in a relationship should have an agreement in place. In particular, if you've been partnered before and there are assets involved that you would like to protect for your children.

The following is a good example of why it's important to get the right advice from the best advisors you can afford.

A husband and wife had been married to each other three times … really … three times! They were worth an absolute bomb. Multiple millions were at stake; they couldn't live together *again* and decided to divorce. The wife was entitled to another huge settlement even though she'd financially wiped the husband out twice before. The husband thought he'd minimised the risk of financial damage by implementing a pre-nup; yet he still had to pay big time!

Prior to the most recent marriage they sought legal advice and put a pre-nuptial agreement in place. The husband believed the potential for financial damage had been limited; yet the wife and her divorce lawyer had other ideas. Due to a fault in the way the agreement had been executed, the courts overturned the agreement and again awarded the wife the significant majority of the accumulated assets.

This is where the *getting the right advice* and *choosing the right adviser* comes in. While the advice was right; the execution was faulty as the solicitor didn't exercise his duty of care to his client or explain fully the financial implications of the documents being signed. If the advice had been executed properly, the amount paid by the husband would have been limited to the amount outlined in the agreement. Instead the husband had to pay far more than anticipated. Now, he's also able to legally pursue the lawyer for damages arising from the cost of the poorly executed advice. Eventually the lawyer's insurer will end up paying the husband's financial losses.

This is a prime example of the importance of getting the most suitable advice to your specific situation *and* working with the best adviser you can afford and find. It's not intended to be sexist; it's intended to illustrate the financial risks of re-partnering.

Are you prepared to take on your new partner at the risk of disinheriting your children? I won't be taking the risk should the need arise.

Tenants in common vs joint tenants

Let me try to clarify the difference between owning something jointly and the legal term 'joint tenants'. Then there's the term 'tenants in common', it's different again. It sounds confusing, yet it's not when you figure it out. (Refer to table on page 139)

To protect a share of joint assets, consider buying large assets, such as property, as tenants in common rather than joint tenants. Purchasing as tenants in common means you can dictate the percentage of an asset that is owned by an individual and can secure entitlements and inheritances.

Ownership can vary anywhere from 1% through to 99%, with the percentage of ownership pre-agreed and allows for more than two people to own the asset. The percentage of ownership is usually recorded in the contract of purchase and is brought into being through the actions of the legal representative responsible for the transfer of ownership at the time of the asset purchase.

Method of ownership	Usual asset types	What happens if you die
Jointly owned	Bank accounts, shares, managed funds	The value of the asset is transferred to the surviving owner following the passing of the other joint owner. The asset becomes the property of the survivor.
Joint tenants	Property	The value of the asset is transferred to the surviving owner following the passing of the other joint owner following proof of death. The asset becomes the property of the survivor.
Tenants in common	Property	The ownership of the asset is specified, usually at time of contract preparation. It clearly stipulates the percentage of ownership attributable to each party. Upon the death of an owner, the percentage owned by the deceased is able to be bequeathed in line with their estate planning wishes

Owning an asset as a tenant in common gives the owner the ability to transfer or bequeath the percentage they own to another person or persons without impacting the percentage of the asset held by the other tenants in common owner or owners.

The power of this arrangement provides assurance in regard to estate planning. Our family home is owned as tenants in common: I own 50% and my partner owns the other 50%. In the event of my passing, my share of the property is to be equally shared amongst our three sons. My partner retains his share; as the property can only be sold with the agreement of all owners, tenancy is assured.

* * *

You insure your homes, cars and health. However, do you, neglect to protect your family against the unexpected? *Surely if the house and car are insured we're fine; we've got the important things covered, right?*

No, you've overlooked something—you and your ability to earn an income and to provide for your family.

There are chronic levels of underinsurance evident in Australia, so thousands of families are at risk of suffering a significant change of circumstance, loss of security or financial losses. How can you minimise the risks your family face? Read on.

Mind Your Money Tip

Be sure you have the correct ownership structure for you. Otherwise you may accidently deprive either yourself or loved ones. Get professional advice to protect yourself.

Chapter 10

Cover Your Financial Butt

'If a child, a spouse, a life partner or a parent depends on you and your income, you need life insurance.'

—*Suze Orman*[18]

Financial professionals don't mean wearing a crash helmet or having air bags in your car when they refer to personal protection. Personal protection is about making sure your biggest asset is insured. Regardless of what you think, or even feel some days, that asset is *you!*

As consumers, we're encouraged to insure items or events; cars, health, home, mobile phone and travel insurance—even funeral insurance. Yet we're seldom encouraged to insure ourselves.

Who's going to look after the bills if you can't?

Too often life insurance is considered too expensive or too hard to get, both are entirely untrue. If you understand the purpose of insurance and what it's intended to do for your family, it's reasonably cheap.

Insurance transfers the risk of something going wrong from you and your family to an insurance company. Insurance is cheap when you consider what you might receive; it's more than the financial benefit.

---

18 www.brainyquote.com

It's the peace of mind you gain from knowing your family's financial security is assured. That feeling is priceless!

Because of Australia's superannuation legislation, there is a widely held belief the insurances inside your superannuation fund will take care of your family if you're no longer around. That's a total fallacy! Most compulsory superannuation insurances do not provide enough cover to allow clearance of the debt levels of most Australians. The average mortgage is around $400,000, yet the average insurance in super is more likely to be $150,000.

Will the covers in your superannuation make your family financially secure? Likely not. Compulsory insurance covers are not as much as most people think.

Most super funds have a set premium (amount paid) for insurances regardless of the member's age. Insurances in super are issued as units of insurance. Members are allocated units, usually two, of life and total and permanent disability covers issued. Because the cost of an insurance unit is capped, the amount of insurance cover reduces depending on the age of the insured. Older members have much less cover than younger members with the same number of insurance units. In these styles of super funds, the insurance you have is based on your age, not on your needs.

Another risk of trusting your super fund to look after your insurance needs is legislation. Super funds can only offer certain types of insurance covers; they legally can't address all risks.

Why insure?

Personal insurances are a trade-off. An individual trades the risk of dying off to an insurance company; if something goes wrong, the insurance company pays up. Insurances are quite cost effective when you consider what you stand to gain and what you are trading off; an annual premium is paid in exchange for a potential lump sum payment.

If you are insured for at least the same amount as your mortgage, you have peace of mind knowing your family can keep the family home if you die. Your family's security is assured; they won't have to keep moving around.

So far we've only considered what happens if you die. There are far more claims for partial disability or medical trauma events than there are for someone passing away, so it's important to have more than just life insurance.

Underinsurance

Have you considered what happens if you have an accident and you live, but you've suffered massive injuries and can never go back to work? I've seen the impact when families are faced with the unexpected. It's emotionally devastating, regardless of whether they're insured, uninsured or underinsured. On the other hand, it can be an immense financial relief if the amount and type of personal insurances are appropriate—financial and emotional burdens can be eased.

The impacts of the unexpected on your family directly relate to the amount of forward planning that's gone before an event.

One case comes to mind: the poor guy simply had to keep working despite the serious back injury and pain he suffered. He was incapacitated, taking huge doses of prescribed opiates to try to manage his pain. He was forced to lie flat in the back of their vehicle as he was transported to worksites. His wife was at the steering wheel with their son beside her, all on their way to the next job. It was necessary so the injured man could supervise his unqualified teenage son to repair the air conditioners he physically couldn't.

Three family members had to 'go to work' to keep income coming in, all because the father had rejected a recommendation to implement income protection cover. He felt the cover was too expensive and couldn't see a need for it. After recovery, he could finally see the value of the recommended cover.

Once recovered he could only get a limited income protection cover; his pre-existing back injury meant the insurer excluded back-related claims from the cover. The exclusion made our client angry; he reasoned if he was paying premiums, the insurer should cover him fully. Cover with exclusions is better than no cover at all; particularly where future financial security could be assured. It was better than being wiped out financially again.

He reluctantly agreed; the risk of suffering another loss of income was transferred to an insurer. Premiums were around 2–3% of his pre-tax income—not a bad trade-off to have 75% of his income replaced is it?

* * *

Oh, wow! Is your head spinning with some of the things you've read so far? I'm pretty sure mine would be if I were you, but I've had many years working in the industry to get used to this.

You're getting a turbo version of all the things learned over more than thirty-five years. Little things like:

* balancing your budget
* reducing your spending by avoiding marketing techniques
* loan refinancing and structuring loans to save *you* money
* ensuring you know the risks of being a guarantor, or disinheriting your children
* how to pay off your loans to your advantage
* how to protect your assets from creditors and predators
* why your family could benefit from you taking out personal insurances.

Next we're going to look at how you can start getting wealthy. Are you ready?

Mind Your Money Tip

Treat your credit rating like it's your reputation—protect it!

Part 3

PROTECT YOURSELF!

Chapter 11

Creating Extra Income Streams

'Start thinking like a millionaire... Package your passions and skills; harness your passions to create multiple streams of income.'
—*Gayle McKew*

Earlier, I discussed the need to create income outside of your working wages, called 'passive income'. There's a strong chance you thought I was crazy. How the heck are you supposed to create a passive income stream when you have no money? Or when you work full time?

Well, the budget exercise in the Foundation chapter is the starting point where you can begin to create passive income. The key to creating wealth is *positive cash flow*.

The best time to start on your investment journey is *now*. Harnessing the power of compounding interest and time is a winning combination.

Passive income

You may have heard people speak of passive income, but you wondered what they mean. We've always been told you have to work hard for our money. Yet when it comes to passive income, this concept couldn't be further from the truth.

According to Wikipedia, 'Passive income is an income received on a regular basis, with little effort required to maintain it'.[19]

This means passive income can be created from a range of assets—assets that provide income with little or no personal exertion required for you to be entitled to the income. Let's consider some sources of passive income:

* *A successful business*, managed by staff, can provide an ongoing income stream with little or no personal input.
* *Royalties* from writing books, songs or from sale of business rights are a form of passive income.
* In these days of e-commerce you can also earn income from *joint ventures* and introductions; the other person does the work, you reap the rewards.
* *Property investments* where you own the whole property or you are part of an investment 'pool' or syndicate[20], which can include residential, industrial or commercial properties, can be leased out to provide an income stream. Collection of the rent and maintenance is usually outsourced, meaning there is little personal input required.
* Direct investment in *company shares that pay dividends* will provide an income stream. As an investor you will receive the financial benefit of how well the management team has performed in managing the business you chose to invest in. Not all company shares pay income, so if you're looking to create an income stream you need to be aware of this when building your share portfolio. Also, unless a company is making a profit it won't be able to pay dividends as dividends generally only come from company profits. If you're thinking of buying a highly speculative stock, possibly involved in exploration or research and development, they generally won't

19 www.en.wikipedia.org/wiki/Passive_income

20 'Pool' in this instance is used to describe a range of investments selected by investment professionals with potential to provide specifically stated invest outcomes for investors. Investments are usually spread across a range of companies as well as investment and market sectors with a view to reducing the levels of risk of total loss within a portfolio.

provide income. The only chance you have of 'winning' with this type of share is if the company makes a major discovery and the concept can be sold for a major profit or is then able to create a future income stream following the discovery.

* *Managed fund portfolios* are often another source of passive income. With these you effectively enter into an agreement to purchase a portion of a 'pool' of investment assets. The 'pool' of assets can include a range of share and/or property investments selected by investment specialists in the asset class/type. In a managed fund the selection of appropriate investments is outsourced to a specialist manager.

  Managed funds generally include a need for the underlying investment to provide income as part of the selection criteria used to create the portfolio. A need to pay all income and dividends to investors is part of the approved investment structure, meaning investors receive an entitlement to income based upon the portion of the investment 'pool' they own. You share income, but have no control over when the manager might sell a part of your investment.
* Interest from *fixed interest and cash investments* held with your bank provide passive income.
* *Annuity or pension income*—these types of investments generally require a lump sum of capital to initially implement the income stream.

We've considered the type of assets that create passive income; now the trick is to figure out just how you too can get a bit of that action for yourself. Let's see what my friend Nicole did.

Creating portfolios

Nicole, who used to waste money, is now committed to saving. She's determined to make up for lost time and is busy considering how she wants to begin investing for her future.

The decision to begin investing was easy, yet when she began trying to figure out what to do next, the choices overwhelmed her.

Nicole struggled to sort through the information available; she didn't have time to sort through it all. The more she dug into it the more difficult it was to make a decision—there was too much to learn. She was paralysed by information overload and fear of making a mistake.

We talked about it and decided her starting point should be to decide what she really wanted the money to do for her in the long term. And to consider how much she wanted to do herself or whether she might be willing to outsource some of the process.

Nicole decided her investment had to: increase in value without relying on additional investment (it needed to have the potential to grow); pay income (she can decide later whether to reinvest or spend the income); allow small regular investments; and to be flexible enough to be accessed fairly quickly in case of an emergency. All of these requirements led us towards an investment in shares, primarily because they provide income, have potential for growth and can be accessed within days if required—ticking the boxes on three of her requirements.

She didn't know anything about shares other than she wanted some; she needed an investment that allowed her to outsource her investment selection. Managed funds do that by providing a pre-selected portfolio, compiled using the skills of investment professionals. Alternatively, if she was determined to use the do-it-yourself (DIY) approach, she needed to find someone willing to provide guidance to assist her to create her own personalised portfolio. A DIY approach would take both time and energy.

She decided she would prefer to have the money working straight away. She decided she would prefer to have the money working straight away and that a pre-selected portfolio of shares in a managed fund was the way to go; it would allow her money to work for her while she set about learning more about investing.

She saved $1000 in her usual bank account to kick-start her investment into a managed fund portfolio. She knew she could save $200 per month by changing her habits; she was willing to use $100 per month to add to her managed fund portfolio. This is called a regular savings plan.

Nicole has decided to 'hang onto' $100 each month to make increased payments on her mortgage.

A little heads up … If you take a DIY approach, you can use the process of regular savings to invest in listed shares too, although you need to be aware most share brokers have a minimum transaction amount. Most brokerage firms also have a minimum transaction amount to access discounts in brokerage costs, otherwise they often will adjust their fees upward until you meet their minimum transaction cost.

Springboard to the future

Nicole decided investing in a managed fund would be a simple way to access the share market; she wanted assets with potential to both pay income and to grow in value. It's part of her much bigger picture … She's planning for the future.

The regular savings strategy is a springboard to much bigger things; like creating a long-term passive income or eventually using part of the accumulated funds as a deposit for a future property purchase. The intention is to start now and decide later. Maybe there will be scope to do both over time. The decision has been made to create a future with choices and greater financial freedom.

The sky is the limit when it comes to future investment opportunities. Nicole identified the importance of taking control; now any restrictions or financial stumbling blocks are likely to come from cash flow limitations (remembering, you need to make more than you spend) or her personal risk tolerance—certainly not from lack of personal interest or knowledge.

Control your money

If you want to be in a position to create the amount of prized passive income we've been talking about, it is vitally important to remember this one little trick: *you control the money; the money does not control you!*

Controlling your money is important; it's the key, both now and in your future. Without controlling your income and expenses now, you will not be able to contribute to your future financial health.

Most people forget they will be forced, at some time in the future, to retire. With retirement comes a loss of your usual income, and that brings a whole range of other challenges to a person who hasn't planned for the future. Challenges like limited income, a change of lifestyle, limited choices and increased health costs.

Your actions now will make a huge difference to your retirement. A little planning now will give you choices; something worth considering.

Mind Your Money Tip

Start planning for your future now.
Results take time. The longer you wait the less time you have to get results!

Chapter 12

Your Longest Holiday

'Retire from work, but not from life.'

—*MK Soni*[21]

The quote says it all. If you want choices in life, start planning, both for now and for how you want to live life when you no longer go to work.

Congratulations. If you're still reading there is a *real* chance you're committed to making a difference to your situation, both now and for the future. It's time for action! Before you start reeling off all the places you want to visit when you retire, *have you started planning how you will afford to have all the things you're dreaming of?* Overseas travel, buying a new car or even a mobile home so you can travel around investigating this beautiful country costs money. Have you thought about how you're going to pay for your longest ever holiday, your retirement?

For many, retirement is a case of survival—a lifestyle with significantly limited choices and one usually heavily reliant on the government-funded age pension entitlements and financial constraints.

From my years as an adviser, a typical retirement plan is all but non-existent. Only as people get closer to retirement do they begin to take an interest in planning for retirement; it's usually only the last year or

---

21 www.retirement-quotes.com/

two before retirement that most people begin to start to plan. Leaving your planning too close to retirement may not end up providing you with greatly improved results, but some planning is much better than no planning. Often the planning happens after the individual finishes working, which can reduce some of the opportunities available to get the best possible outcome.

Would you believe I've been preparing for my retirement since I started working? I'm now fifty-two years old. Initially it was done totally unknowingly; now it's a very deliberate strategy. When I started working, superannuation was compulsory where I worked, but you had to contribute too. I was extra lucky; a very wise person said, 'Sign here', and as a seventeen-year-old I did as I was told. The bonus was every dollar I put in was matched by my employer.

Once I learned the power of superannuation and tax minimisation available when planning for retirement, I planned deliberately.

In fact, through a combination of regular savings (outside of super) and contributing to my superannuation savings, I've been planning for many years now. I want the peace of mind and choices in retirement. Years ago I made a decision not to allow a potential future entitlement to an age pension determine my lifestyle in retirement. Plus, the way the government is playing around with entitlements, the age pension might not be around when I become age eligible. Then where would I be? Being destitute and left with no options is not on my personal agenda.

The inheritance plan

I know some people wait for wealthy family members to die so they can inherit some money to improve their current lifestyle, and possibly their future retirement.

The beneficiary won't fully appreciate the things their loved one might have gone without so they could be sure to leave something for their family. This type of planning can be considered as distasteful, particularly when family members hang around waiting for the loved one to depart this earth. Personally, I'd much prefer to have the loved one in my life.

The lotto plan

You may have some sort of plan: to win lotto, the lottery or the sweepstakes. Sadly the odds of winning a life-changing amount are stacked against you. Let's look at the probability of winning the Saturday Lotto in Australia.[22]

Consider the likelihood of a win in the following prize divisions:

Division	Winning Numbers Required	Probability (Single Game)
1st Division	6	1 in 8 145 060
2nd Division	5 + supplementary	1 in 678 755
3rd Division	5	1 in 36 689
4th Division	4	1 in 733
5th Division	3 + one or both supplementary	1 in 297
6th Division	2 or 1 + 2 supplementary numbers	1 in 144
Any Prize		1 in 85

Remember, by being a regular lotto, lottery or other game of chance player, you may as well throw your money in the air and watch it fly away. It's time for a better plan!

22 www.en.wikipedia.org/wiki/Lotteries_in_Australia

Superannuation

In many countries, the federal government encourages employers, self-employed people and individuals alike to make an effort to save for their retirement. In Australia, such savings are called superannuation. In the US it is referred to as a 401(k) account.

The Australian federal government provides a range of concessions designed to encourage superannuation savings. Thanks to legislation, every Australian employee over the age of 18 will end up with at least one superannuation savings account; this is primarily because it is compulsory for Australian employers to contribute a percentage of an individual's income to a superannuation account.

The government comes to the retirement planning party by providing tax concessions on superannuation accounts. The tax concession sees superannuation savings contributions and earnings taxed at much lower rates than if you kept the money in your usual working account. If you qualify, the government will also provide additional amounts, only after you've done your tax return, to top up your superannuation savings account.

If you contribute funds to your superannuation savings, the government provides some additional protections and tax concessions, with a view to ensuring your retirement nest egg is preserved for when you need it. Such protections can be triggered in the event of a personal bankruptcy; generally your superannuation assets can be protected from a claw back by a bankruptcy trustee.

The only time such a protection won't save your superannuation is if you've manipulated your business books to put more into your super to deprive creditors. The government considers it's fair for you to pay your creditors before you pay yourself, so they will usually authorise release of any excess funds back to your bankruptcy trustee. The offer of protecting your superannuation from a personal bankruptcy trustee may not sound like a lot, but making sure your superannuation can't be accessed by creditors could make a huge difference to your lifestyle in retirement, so it's something for which to be grateful.

The measures outlined above illustrate that it's possible for individuals to save, tax effectively, for their future retirement. Tax effective saving in itself doesn't sound sexy. We are talking about your future retirement and it's about you having lifestyle choices in retirement. Choices in retirement *are* sexy. Ask anyone who doesn't have choices if you don't believe me.

The idea of planning for your retirement is to allow time to accumulate enough assets and money to create a regular income to pay for your longest holiday ever. Without effective planning, you could face very restricted lifestyle choices in retirement.

Super control

This is not about becoming a control freak; it's asking you to take control of your superannuation savings. It's the importance of being diligent about your superannuation.

There are billions of dollars of superannuation sitting in dormant accounts waiting to be claimed by workers who have changed jobs or their address without notifying their superannuation fund. Getting disconnected from your superannuation accounts can happen as simply as that.

The average Australian has three superannuation accounts; however, I've seen clients with as many as 12 super accounts. They kept changing jobs and their new employers kept opening new accounts. It was a nightmare when we decided to try to bring them all together.

Unless you, as an employee, elect to tell your employer where to put your superannuation contributions, the employer is legally required to open a new superannuation account in the employer's default (fall back) superannuation offering. The default fund may not be as good as your current fund; you could be stuck with a fund that is really doing nothing about building wealth for your future.

Superannuation accounts charge ongoing fees to maintain and manage accounts. If you have multiple accounts, then it's safe to assume you will be paying multiple fees—way more than you really need to be paying if you took responsibility and advised your employer of your preferred superannuation fund.

Imagine you took time to streamline the number of superannuation accounts you have, it would reduce the annual paperwork at the very least. You will likely reduce the cost of multiple ongoing fees to a single fee.

You don't have to become a superannuation fund manager to simplify your superannuation. Take an interest in how your money is going to be invested and working for you.

Superannuation is not simply saving for retirement; the Australian government has ensured there are some inbuilt insurance protections. If you are taking time to amalgamate superannuation accounts, be sure you retain the policy or account with the best fees, insurances and conditions for you. If you're unsure of how to go about this, there are fee calculators available on the ASIC Money Smart website (www.moneysmart.gov.au)

Alternatively if the job is too big for you to handle, get professional advice on the best fund for your needs. Professional advisers have an obligation to research your existing funds before rolling them together; they might find a potential advantage for you in keeping a particular superannuation fund that you can't see.

I had a man come to see me because he was sick of having five super funds; he wanted to have a single fund. While discussing his situation he made mention of a pending major back operation. His preference was to have everything 'tidied up' so his super was all together before the operation, in case 'something happened'.

Much to my surprise, there was a very high probability he could end up as a quadriplegic during surgery. My focus changed from meeting his timeline to something entirely different—it became about protecting his existing benefits until the outcome of the surgery was known.

Each of the five superannuation funds had life insurance as well as total and permanent disability insurance as their standard offering. If he rushed to move to a single fund before the operation there was a possibility he could deprive himself of potential insurance payouts of up to $800 000—money that might assist if the worst case scenario he was worried about ended up as the result of the surgery.

This case really proves the importance of understanding the implications of what you might accidently deprive yourself of. Sometimes professional advice really can be worth paying for if it stops you making expensive mistakes.

Effective estate planning

'Estate planning … isn't it just a will?' I've heard people ask. Estate planning doesn't just cover what happens after you've passed; it can work when you're alive too. It is far more than having a will in existence. A will is a written statement indicating how you intend your estate to be distributed; in reality a will is a small part of the big picture of estate planning,

According to Wikipedia, 'Estate planning is the process of anticipating and arranging for the disposal of an estate during a person's life. Estate planning typically attempts to eliminate uncertainties over the administration of probate and maximise the value of the estate by reducing taxes and other expenses. Guardians are often designated for minor children and beneficiaries in incapacity'.[23]

Effective estate planning should consider the use of appropriate strategies and structures to ensure the smooth transition of your assets and personal items to your beneficiaries. It should make provisions in case you can no longer physically or mentally be responsible for your actions while you are alive. Importantly, consider including instructions for managing your health too, not just your assets.

Now while I don't claim to be a legal professional, as part of my life's learnings I've paid for quite a bit of legal advice and know it's important to act while I'm of sound mind. I need to appoint any enduring powers of attorney, appoint guardians for minor children as part of my will and to incorporate the inclusion of testamentary trusts in my will if there is a beneficiary I know will have trouble handling money. It's also important to have legally binding instructions relating to health in place, just in case it's ever needed.

I strongly recommend you get legal advice on what's right for you because estate planning is not something that should be done on a do-it-yourself (DIY) basis. Even though a will kit is initially cheap, taking a DIY stance could end up costing your estate a small fortune. Not to mention being the cause of lots of emotional stress for beneficiaries if it all goes wrong.

The scariest part of not having your estate planning in order well before it is needed is decision making won't always fall to your

23 www.en.wikipedia.org/wiki/Estate_Planning

partner or your family; it could fall to a government department representative. Legal precedents in Australia require an application to the state administrative tribunal for guardianship of a person who has lost capacity.

Loss of capacity relates to a person's loss of ability to make decisions or even to be physically incapable of enacting decisions—think a stroke sufferer or accident victim. An application for guardianship can result in significant stress and unnecessary delays when compared to a bit of pre-planning.

Guardianship applications are not always granted. A state government can, and sometimes does, step in to manage the affairs of a person who no longer has capacity to manage their own affairs; particularly where they (the government) consider the applicant for guardianship is not of suitable character.

If you die without a current will in place, distribution of your estate could end up being done according to a prescribed structure. One such structure would see your estate distributed to your partner, ex-partner if they've borne (had) a child of yours, your children, your parents, your siblings, even your grandparents and so on.

The prescribed structure might end up resulting in the ex-partner you can no longer stand getting their hands on the money you really had planned to leave to your children. That thought alone should be enough to make you get your estate planning in order sooner rather than later.

Estate planning is far more than a will, which outlines who you want to get which of your possessions after you've gone. Other estate planning incorporate documents such as: Enduring Power of Attorney, Guardianship Order, and Advanced Health or Medical Powers of Attorney.

Enduring Power of Attorney

This document allows you to appoint a trusted person or persons to manage your financial situation in the event you aren't able to do it yourself. Depending on the state in which you live, an enduring power of attorney can cover financial matters, general decisions and even your health.

Without an Enduring Power of Attorney, if you suffer a loss of capacity, say from dementia, the government of your state can appoint a guardian to manage your finances. The person appointed may not be the person you would have chosen to act upon your behalf if you had made the decision yourself; in fact, it frequently isn't the person you might have preferred it to be.

Guardianship Order

A guardian's role is the protection of interests of a person without capacity. They are generally appointed by the courts. The guardian has an obligation to protect the assets of the individual no longer capable of making their own decision.

Where joint assets are held it can result in not being able to sell assets at all, simply because the guardian has an obligation to protect the assets of the person without capacity. This can have dire consequences for the other owner of the asset, or possibly even the person needing a guardian if the asset could have been sold and the proceeds used to provide a better quality of care than is available without accessing those funds.

My mother's neighbours didn't plan ahead. The man was secretive and hid his advancing dementia for many years. The woman was from a non-English speaking background and was scared to seek help; instead she tried to manage their situation the best she could—she paid their bills and organised their lives.

While caring for her husband, the woman had a stroke that took away her capacity. Their daughter was in the unenviable position of having both of her parents needing care, yet unable to legally make decisions. She was forced to apply for a Guardianship Order for each of her parents.

Her application for guardianship was denied because the daughter intended to sell the family home and use the capital to pay for the care her parents now needed. The government department decided selling the family home wouldn't be 'preserving' the assets of the concerned parties (her parents) and would deprive the beneficiaries of the estate.

The situation was crazy: the only beneficiary was the daughter. By making it impossible to sell the family home, the family were forced into paying unnecessary interest charges and other fees relating to her parents' care.

This true story illustrates how damaging and far reaching not having such important documents in place can be. Get in contact with your solicitor to ensure your family isn't impacted by lack of planning.

Advanced Health Directive or Medical Powers of Attorney

These documents/facilities are not available in all states. These documents provide clear instructions to your doctor, your attorneys and your family regarding the types of care you are willing to accept in relation to your health.

Our family had been operating with a clear understanding between a family member's doctor and the family regarding health matters due to early stages of dementia. When the original doctor retired, the new practice manager advised previous arrangements would no longer be honoured; they would only speak with a person holding a power of attorney.

The practice manager was on the right track even though she used the wrong term to refer to the document. What she was telling me was 'we need legal documentation that shows you have a right to provide instructions and to be provided with personal information'. If there are known health preferences or religious concerns, get help from a solicitor to make formal arrangements; you never know when they might be needed.

If you find your loved one in hospital suffering a life-threatening illness, medical staff will want to preserve their life and may take no notice of verbal preferences. My own mother has no intention of accepting artificial life support; her preference is to be allowed to pass pain-free and with dignity. We needed appropriate legal documentation to confirm her instructions, otherwise her wishes could be overruled. A legal advisor confirmed she was of sound mind prior to formalising the instructions. All of the family are aware of her wishes, which rules out disputes—another risk that can be removed by implementing the correct documentation and having clear instructions.

Some families find planning and discussing health-related matters to be distasteful. It pays to have formalised arrangements if religious views and practices need to be considered. I've had clients whose religion does not allow blood transfusions. Rather than risk a forced transfusion, they decided to implement the documents so they could clearly outline their preferences to medical professionals.

Going DIY and getting it wrong

Yes, estate planning can be done on a DIY basis, though I do not recommend it. Getting it wrong comes with potential for financial disaster. It's particularly weird that we think we can use a DIY method when there's evidence the professionals in this field can still get it wrong.

Using a DIY will kit can appear to be the cheapest alternative to paying a solicitor to draw up your will. bit a DIY approach to estate planning is fraught with potential problems, many of which can result in expensive legal challenges. I know a number of legal professionals who say a DIY will is generally open to challenge, and a licence to print money for the professional launching the challenge.

Paying a solicitor to prepare your will could be *the* most cost-effective option available to your estate in the long run.

A professional legal adviser reduces the chances of a successful challenge to your estate. They know the potential points of challenge and will take steps to ensure your will is created to accommodate your wishes as well as reduce the risk of any potential challenges to the way your estate is distributed. Most people are unaware a challenge to the distribution of your estate is paid for by your estate before any beneficiaries get a single cent. The person challenging the distribution of your wealth does not pay a cent; your estate foots the bill.

There is an ever-increasing potential for unhappy beneficiaries or people who think they should have a claim on your estate to instigate a challenge. Legal eagles are probably rubbing their hands together in excitement at the prospect of challenging estates.

There are many horror stories that you might be aware of where families are fighting over money after a loved one has died. A family in rural New South Wales had an estate distribution challenged because a single person perceived they had been treated unfairly.

The challenger thought they had an entitlement to their estranged mother's estate. The whole family knew the story of how and why he'd already been disowned and disinherited by the family; the challenger had previously ripped off their parents for around $500 000 years before. As the challenger wasn't mentioned in the mother's will, nor had the reasons why they had been excluded from the will been noted anywhere (ideally this should be in the will and in the legal advisors file notes), the apparently disinherited person was advised to challenge the validity of the will.

After ripping off the parents, from a moral perspective alone the family felt they should have no right to benefit from the estate. The reality was far different.

In Australia, the Family Provisions Act 1982 states there is provision to challenge the distribution of a deceased estate where there is an expectation of being a beneficiary and there is subsequent exclusion. Because of the act, the door was wide open for the disgruntled excluded 'beneficiary' to challenge the will.

The challenge was a long drawn out saga; much longer and more expensive than anyone could ever have imagined. Initially, six beneficiaries were mentioned and the estate was just short of $6 million. Each beneficiary should have received in excess of $900 000 after costs were met. Because of bad advice and structuring, what sounded like a great windfall didn't end up that way for the intended beneficiaries.

After multiple protracted disputes, what could have been a relatively simple sharing of the asset pool didn't happen. The original beneficiaries could have added the 'black sheep' to the beneficiary list, with each beneficiary then receiving in the order of $770 000. Instead they agreed to disagree. You could almost hear the solicitor's cash registers ringing.

The challenge took many years; the asset pool kept shrinking. Eventually they agreed to distribute. Each of the seven beneficiaries received only around $100 000, a far cry from the original $900 000 or even the $770 000 they would have received if they'd agreed to share with the 'black sheep'.

The cost of all the challenges had resulted in the asset pool falling from close to $6 million to $700 000. The moral of the story is: Get it right the first time. But if you can't get it right, work to limit the potential for damage.

I encourage you to start making decisions on who you want things to go to when you're no longer around and who you want to make decisions relating to your assets and health when you can't make those decisions for yourself. It's tough to make a decision that might offend a loved one ... just take a deep breath, make a decision and get something in writing before it's too late.

Grab the phone book and call the solicitor of your choice; it's time to get the ball rolling.

What's not covered by your will

When I mentioned the terms 'estate assets' and 'non-estate assets' to a friend, they thought I was speaking another language. 'What's the difference? You'd better explain', they said.

We looked at the importance of getting your estate planning right earlier; however, here's a quick heads-up. Some things you consider to be yours won't be treated as part of your estate. Your will doesn't cover everything you own or think of as yours.

Estate assets are items you own personally and can bequeath to people through your will. Non-estate assets are a totally different story; they are entirely outside of the scope of your will and are dealt with separately from your estate.

Let's consider a few:

* *Jointly owned assets* (remember we talked about joint tenants earlier) like bank accounts, property, shares, managed funds, vehicles, collectables and pretty much everything else you own jointly become the property of the survivor. Joint tenancy (ownership) means you can't leave your 'share' of the asset

pool to any other person; your death is the trigger to transfer your share of those jointly owned assets to the survivor.

* Your *superannuation* is not automatically a part of your estate. The trustees of your super fund will be responsible for determining the eventual beneficiaries of your superannuation entitlements. They do this after considering things like binding death nominations and claims from people who consider they have an entitlement to your superannuation i.e. your current partner, your ex-partner or your children.

  As a last resort it's possible for the proceeds of your superannuation to end up in your estate, but that's fairly rare unless your binding nomination say it's to go there. Having your superannuation included as part of your estate is *not* something you should count on.

  Trustees have to give consideration to all claimants, so your super funds could end up going where you don't really want them to go if you don't keep beneficiary nominations up to date.

  I know of superannuation monies going to a much despised ex-wife because the man hadn't updated his beneficiaries. His heavily pregnant new partner claimed on his super, only to have her claim denied. The ex-wife benefited thanks to a binding nomination; they last for a minimum of three years unless revoked.

* If you have a *family trust,* trust assets aren't yours to bequeath; they are the assets of the trust and belong to the trust beneficiaries en masse. It is entirely outside of your ability to control what happens with trust assets even if you mention them in your will.
* If the trust uses a corporate trustee structure and you are a director of the corporate trustee, you can bequeath your shares in the trustee company, just not the assets of the trust.
* Your family company assets aren't yours to bequeath through your will either. They are the assets of the company and effectively belong to the company shareholders. You can bequeath your shares in a company, not the assets of the company.

* * *

You may feel like you've been on an information roller coaster; there's so much to take in. And why have I talked about so many seemingly unrelated topics as estate planning and superannuation, STDs and personal protection, habits and spending?

The intention was to draw your attention to how seemingly unrelated things can be directly related to how you make decisions and buy things … and who you might accidently disinherit.

Knowing this seemingly unrelated information can help as you draw together information and assets will help with mapping out your master plan. Are you ready to create your future?

Mind Your Money Tip

Start planning now so you don't have to retire from life when you retire. And make sure your estate planning is prepared for the unexpected!

Chapter 13

Create a Master Plan

'Plans are nothing; planning is everything.'

—Dwight D. Eisenhower

Most of us have a general idea of goals we want to achieve, like:

* a new car or a holiday every year
* to own your own home
* to see your family financially secure
* to not have to work
* to maybe buy an investment property, or maybe much, much more.

It's great to have goals, yet most people don't actually achieve their goals simply because they don't have a written action plan to help achieve them.

Having a plan sounds boring, yet it's important to have a well-structured plan to assist you along your journey. A good plan can assist with:

* goal setting
* learning to live within your means

* setting milestones, like how much and by when
* giving you measurable outcomes.

Why a Master Plan?

Many think we can do this type of planning ourselves. But do we actually do anything about articulating our plans clearly? You know—putting pen to paper. We talk about doing something, yet most won't do anything but talk because we don't know the steps required to make it possible to reach a goal.

For some, creating a written plan seems way too hard; we don't know where to start or more to the point we're lacking the discipline to actually get started. Oh, we're all guilty of a little procrastination at some time in our lives, me included; the key is not to be so crippled by procrastination you do nothing.

Consider the following if you would like to be successful:

* Create a list of goals.
* Match those goals to suitable time frames.
* Decide how you are going to achieve what's on your list.
* Consider whether the items on the list are truly achievable.
* If they aren't achievable, consider what steps you might need to take to improve the likelihood for success.
* Define the actions required to make your goals achievable or go back and refine those goals.
* Consider if cash flow supports you in achieving your stated goals? If not, what is required to make it happen and turn things into reality?

The table on the next page is an example 'wish list' of a young couple and gives you an idea of the types of questions to ask yourself.

If these people were my clients and they were seeking my advice professionally, I would begin by asking them to tell me *why* each item is important; to understand what makes them tick and what *truly* is their priority, or if the priority was possibly created by someone else.

The couple have about $18 000 in savings and $3000 in credit card debt. They are determined to build a home worth about $450,000 because they don't want to miss out on the government grants available. They want their own home because all of their friends seem to be buying and they don't want to be the odd ones out.

The overseas holiday started out as a 'not negotiable' item, yet they decided it could wait if they weren't going to be able to buy a house. It turns out they were planning the trip because their friends were going. The investment property is still on the wish list with an extended time frame.

Next would be to create a list of items for consideration and discussion; to find out how much they know about what they intend to do. While they know what they want, it's important to understand what they know about how to go about it.

Do they know and understand:

* the cost of keeping the credit card debt
* the interest earned on the account is taxable
* how much deposit is required for the house
* the process of buying a house
* lenders' mortgage insurance and who it protects.

Goal	Time frame	Cost	Level of importance	Negotiable/ Not negotiable
Buy a home	1 year	$450 000	High	Negotiable on time frame
Pay off credit cards	2–3 years	$3000	Low	Not negotiable
Overseas holiday	6 months	$6000	High	Not negotiable
Investment property	2 years	$350 000	Medium	Negotiable on time frame

The credit card

What they know: The interest rate is 13.95% per annum; they are paying the minimum payment when it's due.

Action: Make them aware they're paying a large amount of interest on the credit card. At a rate of 13.95% per annum, in simple terms the interest cost, assuming nothing was repaid off the debt, would be $418.50 per annum. By only making minimum repayments, according to Money Smart, they would take 16 years and 11 months to pay off the debt, with repayments totalling $6207 during that time.

To clear the debt in the two years they had planned, they would need to pay monthly amounts of $142, with repayments totalling $3416.

The cost of keeping the credit card (annual fee) and paying interest and annual fees would not be tax deductable.

The conduct of how they had managed the credit card will be considered when they apply for a loan and the limit ($5000) would be included in calculations to assess their eligibility for a loan. If the credit card debt was repaid it would probably make it easier to afford the loan for the planned property purchase.

The savings account

What they know: Their savings is earning 3.0% per annum.

Action: Raise awareness that earnings on accounts are taxable income and will be taxed at their own tax rates.

If they considered using $3000 of their savings to clear the credit card debt, they would 'miss out' on $90 per annum in earned interest while saving $418.50 in interest charges. This is a much better alternative than paying interest on the outstanding debt.

Additionally, they would be able to increase the amount they are saving by no longer having to meet loan repayments on the credit card debt.

More than a deposit

What they know: You can borrow up to 95% of the value of the property.

Action: Turn this knowledge into numbers; it makes it more real.

If they buy a $450 000 property, they need a minimum of 5% deposit plus costs (legal and stamp duty costs) available to them. The government grant they spoke of applies to newly constructed properties—the grant is a 'building boost' designed to stimulate the building industry.

They plan on buying an existing property so won't be eligible for the grant; as a result they will need to have access to $22 500 (the 5% deposit) plus the cost of conveyancing (legal) and stamp duties relating to the transfer of property. As they are first home owners, the stamp duty cost is currently discounted and in the order of $1120 in Queensland at the time of writing. They will also need to meet conveyancing costs, which are likely to be in the order of $1200.

Overall, to be able to complete the purchase of a $450 000 property they will need access to at least $24 820 of their own money *plus* a loan of $427 500 from a friendly lender.

They were stunned. They hadn't known about the stamp duty or legal costs and now realise they need to save a bit longer if they are to buy a property.

They have $18 000 and save $200 per week, so it will take another 34 weeks to save the additional funds, assuming they don't pay off the credit card. If the credit card is paid off it will take them 15 weeks to achieve the amount required to cover their deposit, legal costs and stamp duty. Paying off the credit card first seems to be the quickest way to achieve their goals.

The process of buying

What they know: They need a solicitor, a real estate agent and a loan from the bank.

Action: Raise awareness of the steps to buying a property.

Know your budget and preferred buying range. It's fine for the bank to say you can 'afford' to spend $500 000, but do you really want to? Most first time property buyers get a little overwhelmed and find themselves emotionally involved in the purchase. Put your business hat on instead. You're going to be paying the loan off for a long time; now is time to make sharp decisions.

I've always taken a slightly different view with property than most; I make an offer *much* lower than the asking price to show interest then wait. If my offer interests the vendor (seller) they can make a counteroffer or tell me my offer isn't interesting enough. Either way, it's a great way to gauge the vendor's interest in selling. We've bought all but two of our properties using this method; the other two were bought at auction, which is another story altogether. Every cent you don't spend is less to pay off and less interest you'll pay to the bank.

If you are at the signing contracts stage you should be aware of information you can use to protect yourself; it turns out a lot of people don't realise it's possible to protect themselves at contract stage.

Essential protections are ensuring your contract has a cooling off period and having an 'escape' clause or two built in, although none of this applies if you buy at auction. The usual terms used for 'escape' clauses are specific, are noted on the contract and are likely to be listed as *subject to pest and building inspection* and *subject to finance approval*. The 'escape' clauses are not because you're not committed; rather it's in case of structural or pest problems with the property you've fallen in love with. Plus you need time to ensure you can source finance. Lenders need time to process a loan application if you haven't pre-arranged finance.

While I'm not a legal eagle, I have signed enough contracts to know sometimes the exit clause/cooling off period is exercised. There's a thing called 'contract law' that might see you litigated against (sued) if you don't complete the purchase, especially if escape clauses weren't included and exercised properly.

As you probably aren't a legal specialist, it's recommended you appoint a solicitor or conveyancing specialist to complete the transfer for you. I always do as I really don't want to be responsible for making potentially costly mistakes by trying to do it myself!

Size matters

What they know: It's possible to borrow up to 95% of the price.

Action: Raise awareness of loan sizes and the potential need for Lender's Mortgage Insurance.

The size of your loan depends on the deposit you have to put towards the purchase price. As a rule of thumb, lenders will lend up to 80% of the purchase price without asking for Lender's Mortgage Insurance (LMI). Borrowing above 80% of the value of the proposed property will see you pay LMI. Lenders are at times willing to advance up to 95% of the purchase price. Contributing factors to their decision include but aren't restricted to: the postcode, population size, likelihood of employment and loan size (in terms of percentage) compared to the asset value (purchase price).

In some instances the lender will allow the LMI to be added to your loan amount, referred to as capitalising LMI. In others, the LMI premium has to be paid separately. Whether you pay or capitalise LMI depends on the total percentage of borrowing after capitalisation of the LMI premium.

Lender's mortgage insurance (LMI)

What they know: Nothing.

Action: Make them aware of why they pay LMI.

LMI protects the bank in the event the borrower defaults on the loan. If they don't pay, the bank has a right to sell the property to recover what it's owed. In the event there is a shortfall between what the property sells for and what is owed, the bank makes a claim on the LMI cover they paid for.

LMI involves a one-off payment with the cost of the premium not able to be recovered if the bank doesn't need to make a claim. LMI is specific to the lender and cannot be transferred if you decide to refinance your borrowings with another lender.

Summary

They decided:

* The credit card will be repaid from savings immediately—ahead of schedule.
* Even with paying off the credit card the goal of buying a house is on track—they decided to start looking around in around ten months' time, knowing they will be able to buy within 12 months—on schedule.
* The overseas holiday is off the table.
* The investment property now has an extended time frame, three to four years, now they understand the process of buying and the need to save a deposit or access equity if their home increases in value.

Use basically the same principles when deciding on investments: Break down each goal, assess the likelihood of success in your stated time frame, and start researching options and preferred ways of entering a specific style of investment market. Knowledge is power … The more you know the better decisions you make.

If you aren't able to break down the processes required to any strategy, it could be time to get yourself a 'coach', one who will get you on track and care about your results.

Get a coach

If you lack discipline, or even know-how, this is where you need a financial coach to help you lay out your plan and achieve your goals.

Serious athletes want to be *the very best* in their discipline. Smart, focused athletes quickly realise they can't do it all—there are too many 'things' to research and control. If they focus on 'things' they won't have time to work on performance.

Athletes employ coaches and implement training regimes; meaning the athlete's goal becomes a team goal. They are no longer accountable just to themselves; there are coaches to answer to and they try harder until they master the skills and discipline to achieve their dream.

When it comes to our finances, most are too lazy or disorganised to get started. Without a coach there is absolutely no accountability for your financial performance.

If you are serious about achieving your goals, consider getting yourself a financial coach or financial planner. It will be their job to keep you on track. One suggestion though—choose your financial coach wisely.

I've been in social situations—barbecues, dinner parties, family gatherings and even business meetings—and overheard well-meaning people sprouting investment advice. Every time I overhear these conversations I shudder, particularly when I consider the implications of some of the advice.

Advice usually comes from well-meaning friends, neighbours and family members, all of whom are happy to give you their advice and opinion, regardless of whether you asked for it or not. Sometimes you've asked for it, other times it's been foisted upon you because they love to hear their own voice. While the advice is generally well intentioned, it's worthwhile checking a few key things before following recommendations.

Who's your advisor?

If you're planning to be your own adviser and tapping into the vast array of advice on the internet or from well-meaning family and friends, you will need to be careful to filter potential good advice from bad.

Assess whether the advice and opinions have a reasonable likelihood of being sound. Decide if the advice could put you on the road to success or disaster by checking out the following:

* their track record
* if they understand your situation
* if the risk is appropriate for your situation
* if there is an ulterior motive.

What's their track record?

Often people may not have a good track record of personal investment; they just have an opinion. Frequently they have a record of poor personal financial management and don't understand the difference between good debt and bad debt. Often they have large amounts of personal debt with nothing but the latest electronic gadgets and toys to show for it.

Remember, well-intended advice counts for nothing when you're the one losing your money. It's worth remembering not all risks are worth taking.

Check to see if they have actually created their own investment or property portfolio. If not, their advice is likely groundless. The person who's just given you advice at the barbecue may have no qualifications or even experience relating to investing. Are you willing to take that sort of advice?

Do these so-called advisors understand your situation? This isn't very likely, particularly if you've met in a social situation. Most people don't bring personal balance sheets to a party, so there's no chance your potential adviser could know the ins and outs of your finances. They also won't have given any consideration as to the impact on your personal financial situation in the longer term. They don't have to; they're not the one who will pay the price if things go wrong—you will.

Not all risks are the same

Not all risks are the same: some can be catastrophic, some cause barely a ripple, yet others come with rewards. Know the level of risk you're willing to take and stay in your zone.

Consider if the risk is appropriate to your situation and if the risk is in proportion to the reward you might receive. If the risk isn't suitable, either in proportion to your overall portfolio or to your personal risk tolerance (whether you are willing to risk losing the amount or not), then simply leave the opportunity alone for now. It's the safest way to proceed until you build your skills and knowledge.

We all need to learn to take appropriate levels of risks when making investment decisions. Yet the level of risk each person is willing to take usually relates to their personal experience and knowledge levels. Acceptance and tolerance of risk is not a 'one size fits all' solution.

Is there an ulterior motive?

You might be surprised to know how much profit can be made from building a property if you are a developer, builder or property promoter. Real estate agents make commissions on property sales—it's disclosed and is widely known. The seller knows roughly what the cost of the real estate commission will be before they list the property for sale.

Yet many property promoters receive undisclosed benefits from the sale of a property. How can that be? Often arrangements are made between the property promoter, developer and builder that are off public record. This ensures the property promoter receives a reward for bringing the developer and builder additional business.

In some businesses the goal is to find unsuspecting buyers, preferably from out of town, to sell to. I was horrified when I discovered a company I used to work for was doing this. Unsuspecting buyers would be flown in for the weekend, shown multiple blocks of land plus property layouts, and kept too busy to research options. There was lots of pressure to have buyers sign contracts before they realised they were in the process of being fleeced.

For every property sold, developers would pay my employer $30 000 under the table. Plus clients paid a buyer's fee for the privilege of buying through my employers. The goal was two properties per client. It turned out to be quite the payday for my boss.

To this day, many of those clients still love the man; luckily others managed to see through him. It was incredibly confronting to discover I was working for such a business. My ethics meant I was out of there quick smart. Selling artificially inflated property is, in my view, entirely unethical.

The cost of this type of undisclosed payment is built into the purchase price paid by an unsuspecting buyer. I shared this to encourage buyers to make conscious decisions, it's super important to know just what you're paying for when buying property.

It's not always clear when you might be taken advantage of, so keep your eyes open. Someone with an ulterior motive isn't always a stranger … sometimes the person taking advantage can appear to be a 'friend'.

We were having dinner with friends. Excitedly they shared they'd been given a huge opportunity—to provide a temporary loan to the new partner of a long standing and trusted friend. Our friends weren't too excited about making the loan, but the interest rate had them very excited. It would be short term; the intended borrower promised to pay a 50% return on the borrowed amount. My internal alarm bells started ringing … loudly!

They'd recently received an inheritance; otherwise they wouldn't have been able to consider making the loan. The new partner of their friend had asked for a loan term of three months. Our friends would receive $15 000 for providing a loan of $30 000; no wonder they were excited. While the friend had earned their trust, the new partner had done no such thing—they'd met him twice!

I broke my personal rule of never providing advice in a social situation. My usual response is to tell a person to come see me in the office where I can truly investigate their financial position. In this instance I cautioned our friends to only provide the loan if they were willing to lose the entire capital amount, along with the long-term friend, if things went horribly wrong.

Two months later the friends thanked me. They'd just found out the new partner had been in court and was being sued for significant amounts. Their money had been intended to pay off the plaintiff. The new partner ended up in jail and the friend's money would have been lost forever.

Can you afford to risk it?

Just after Dad retired, he informed me he'd sent off for documents for an investment he'd seen advertised on television. The rate of return was twice what the bank was paying and Dad had decided he wanted some of that action.

I told him I wanted to investigate the quality of the investment before he put any money into the investment—it didn't go down well. Next visit he thrust a document at me; a quick perusal showed me what we needed to know. The document included the balance sheet of the company, which showed the investment would be extremely high risk. The company was a front for a property development cartel that could no longer raise money from traditional sources like banks. I told Dad to only put as much money into the 'investment' as he would be willing to throw out into the street; the risk was very high and the capital would be lost regardless of the promise of a very high interest rate.

He was not a happy chappie—an upstart daughter was telling him what he could or couldn't do with his money. I was in trouble! If looks could kill I'd be pushing up daisies instead of writing this.

Because I am my father's daughter, I was really worried he'd ignore me and go ahead regardless. Thankfully, he decided to take notice of my explanation and didn't invest. Three months later the company went into liquidation and investors lost all invested capital. By electing not to participate in this 'opportunity', my parents retained their capital. Sadly other investors, many retirees, lost capital, with those losses directly and adversely impacting the lifestyle quality of those who lost money.

Whose goals are you using?

Let me tell you the story about a couple who had huge plans.

A newly engaged couple were in my office, reviewing their investments. They were in the early stages of creating investment portfolios and still learning about the importance of budgeting and risks. They were excited to advise they had a 12 month plan. On the list was:

* getting married
* having a baby

* buying their dream home—they'd already been checking out properties.

I congratulated them on having a plan. I could see a few tiny flaws, but there was a plan. I was excited; we had a starting point and something to work with. We looked at their plan in detail:

* The baby part was non-negotiable. The rush was brought about by an extremely loudly ticking biological clock.
* Getting married was also a non-negotiable. Religion and personal preferences meant they would be married before having a baby.
* How they got married was negotiable. They'd been considering a grand production for their wedding; after consideration, a small and intimate wedding better suited their plans. They chose to focus only on family and close friends, rather than having a huge wedding production designed to impress an extended group of friends and acquaintances.
* Owning a home turned out to be negotiable. It wasn't really their goal; it was a borrowed goal. The home-buying goal arose from family pressures and expectations; both sets of parents expected them to buy a home when married. When asked why, the only answer available was because it was what their parents had done.

The cost of buying a home some 35 years ago compared to now is very different. The average house in Brisbane in 1980 cost $35 475[24], so a house on the Gold Coast would have cost less than $30 000; whereas a median house price in Brisbane in 2010 was $500 000.[25] Long term affordability of owning property was very different for this couple compared to their parents.

The flaws in the plan were around housing; they hadn't taken into consideration some important factors:

---

24 www.econ.mq.edu.au/Econ_docs/research_papers2/2004_research_papers/Abelson_9_04.pdf

25 www.brisbanetimes.com.au/queensland/queensland-property/median-house-price-surges-past-500000-20100308-pqt3.html

* They had about 5% of the proposed purchase price as capital. The remainder of the purchase price and related costs would have to be borrowed.
* They would pay more to cover the cost of interest-only repayments than if they continued renting.
* Interest-only loan repayments would simply be helping their lenders bottom line; they would not be creating equity in the property.
* They couldn't afford to make principle and interest repayments on the loan size they would need.
* They would have increased costs associated with land rates and property insurances, something renters don't have to worry about.
* The wife would be taking unpaid maternity leave, which would make the prospect of affordability even more difficult.
* Trying to live on a single income with the prospect of increased costs was not viable.

I outlined my concerns: it would leave them struggling. They would be trying to stretch a single wage to pay a mortgage while also paying regular transport, phone and utility bills, buy clothes and support a new baby, and they still needed to eat. It would have to be done on about $70 per week after paying the mortgage; they realised it would be impossible.

They were extremely unhappy. Their dream home was disappearing before their eyes and I was the 'bad guy' for pointing out the pitfalls in the plans.

Next meeting saw matching wedding bands and a baby bump on display. They'd ticked two of three items off their wish list/plan. I was quite surprised when they thanked me for the reality check I'd provided at our last meeting.

They hadn't liked the reality check at the time but acknowledged the advice they hadn't wanted to hear was sound. It was hard to make ends meet on a single wage and they'd decided to move in with family to get through the financially tough period.

By not buying a house they could make other important lifestyle choices regarding their family. Without financial pressures, they could choose for one of them to work on a part-time basis until all children were school age; it was a core value for at least one parent to be present in the lives of their children until they went to school.

The moral of the story is to have a plan but be prepared to tweak it to meet ever-changing goals and personal objectives. A professional financial planner can help you with this.

Mind Your Money Tip

A written plan is a tool to measure your progress. Without it you're just guessing!

Chapter 14

Work With a Professional

'Successful and unsuccessful people do not vary greatly in their abilities. They vary in their desires to reach their potential.'

—John Maxwell[26]

We use professionals for all sorts of things and for all sorts of reasons. It's times when you can't afford for things to go wrong when you decide to use a professional adviser.

Professionals usually specialise in a specific area of your life: they do the job more effectively and save you time and sometimes money. They're the people you call on for help with a range of services and advice you can't do yourself. Would you ask a local health care professional to perform intricate brain surgery? No. It's understandable to exercise such caution when things are too important to mess with—like your finances.

Choosing your trusted professional

Professional advisers take time to understand your objectives; helping you to understand and dissect goals, breaking them into workable and achievable sections and measuring progress against your stated goals.

---

26 www.brisbanetimes.com.au/queensland/queensland-property/median-house-price-surges-past-500000-20100308-pqt3.html

They're savvy enough to recognise potential problems and stumbling blocks, even problems not relating directly to their area of expertise. It's not possible for every adviser to know everything, nor is it possible for them to be licensed to provide advice in all areas. If your adviser is limited by a licence and specific legislative restrictions, they will have to *refer you* to other qualified professionals with the expertise required. When you are referred to a specialist in another area of expertise, you can usually rest assured you are being referred to another trusted professional.

I'm only willing to refer to another professional after we have established and built a trust relationship. If you are provided with a referral to another professional, consider they've already passed one trust test. You still need to cast your own trust test over each prospective adviser; they have to earn your trust too.

Most people have aspects of their financial life that could do with attention if they want the best possible outcomes. Assuming money is money and you can't change the way you do things is wrong. Yes, money is money, yet there are many ways you can adapt and change the way you use money so it's creating an advantage for you. This is one reason to use a professional; they can teach you new ways of operating.

There are constant changes being made to the financial services legislation. Every time a federal budget is handed down there are far reaching implications for the community; without you even being aware of it, you too will be impacted by the changes.

By taking a do-it-yourself position you will have your work cut out keeping up with the ongoing changes; it's a full-time pursuit just to figure out how to maximise some of the advantages in your favour. Financial professionals have an obligation to stay abreast of these constant changes, using the constant changes to evolve and adapt advice, allowing you to take advantage of any benefits available.

Benefits of the right advice

I use other professionals for specific aspects of my own financial life; there are areas where others' skills exceed my own, such as specific accounting and legal advice.

The initial cost of seeking professional advice is usually relatively small when compared to long term outcomes. Outcomes have been improved after implementing the right advice.

If you could access a service to ultimately provide significantly improved results would you do it? Of course! But what if there was an upfront cost you had to pay before you could benefit from the service? Most people baulk at paying up front, yet the *future* results are going to provide serious long-term benefit.

Here's how our accountant helped. The actual cost of getting structural advice has been significantly outweighed by the financial benefits to our family. We paid $1000 for advice: relating to using the correct investment structure for legal tax minimisation. Since implementing the advice, we have benefited from tax savings amounting to many tens of thousands of dollars compared to what we would have paid personally. Because of the advice, our tax savings are on-going. The advice will continue to provide financial benefit for years to come.

The initial cost of $1000 for advice is a drop in the ocean when compared to the savings we receive, and the cost of advice was tax deductible. The price was definitely worth paying upfront.

Communication is key

When choosing a professional to work with it is important to create an ongoing trust; without trust, relationships are doomed to failure. Make sure you can communicate freely with your adviser, and the communication needs to be two way. Your adviser needs to be able to tell you the truth, especially when actions are detrimental to the overall plan, without fear of termination.

You should also be able to trust that your adviser has your best interests at heart. If you don't feel this is the case, it's time to discuss the situation. If all else fails, it's time to find another trusted adviser.

Seek a professional opinion on your own situation; if nothing else, consider a meeting with a financial professional as a second opinion, one who will allow you to see if you really are on track. If you're not on track, there are many strategies available to assist you to improve your current circumstances.

At times clients and I don't always share the same opinion on a strategy; they think it's working well and I can see why it's not. The same can apply to couples, where each has a significant difference in understanding of risk tolerance (how much they are willing to lose); they often benefit from a third viewpoint or different explanation. Differences of opinion can be major disruptions to relationships. Sometimes the difference of opinion is because of miscommunication and pre-existing conditioning. Other times, fear and a lack of information or knowledge relating to a topic can cause confusion and disagreement.

I've had a husband and wife bitterly arguing over investing in shares. They were so used to fighting they weren't really listening to each other. I remember explaining share investing to the woman. She promptly turned to her husband demanding, 'Why didn't you explain it like that?' All I did differently was add a few hand-drawn diagrams and language she could connect with. Share investing went from being a no-go zone to very acceptable quick smart!

Other times clients have changed their minds, stating they were no longer willing to do what was recommended. With one set of clients we had been working to reduce aged-care fees and to get a part-pension for the family matriarch when suddenly it appeared that this was no longer important. Rather than becoming offended, I asked what caused the change of heart.

It was an internal family dispute. One family member wanted to buy the family home (super cheap of course). Others weren't keen on that and they were plotting options to undermine the potential buyer.

Without buying into family politics, I explained what they were considering would be the worst possible outcome for the family matriarch. There were other options to provide what the family needed and wanted to achieve.

Armed with full information, they could make empowered decisions to benefit the matriarch. The best outcome had an unintended side effect—it took the heat out of the family dispute.

What advisers might do

Professional advisers all have their own way of doing things. What they need to know determines the types and depth of questions they will ask.

Some professionals are influenced by a legislated need to know everything about your personal situation before providing advice—this applies to financial planners. Other professionals, such as barristers, may not ask for details. A barrister explained he never wanted to know of a client's guilt because, if the client confessed, the barrister would be unable to represent his client. Talk about professional differences!

When asking an advisor to provide financial guidance, lots of questions will be asked so they are able to give full consideration to your situation. A few things a professional adviser might discuss are: your goals, tax efficiencies and implications, cash flow, your assets.

Your goals

First, an adviser can determine whether your goals are achievable and realistic. If they're not the adviser usually offers a range of suitable alternatives that may be achievable with a bit effort.

Tax efficiencies and implications

What tax implications? In Australia, unless we're talking about your principle place of residence (the home in which you live) there will be some sort of tax implications arising from each investment decision. Leaving money sitting in your bank account earning interest has tax implications.

A professional adviser will be aware of things like personal tax rates, capital gains tax, whether you should be making the investment in your personal name, using an investment structure or even superannuation as your investment vehicle. Generally, they recommend strategies that offer improved tax outcomes when compared to DIY investing.

Cash flow

Professionals aren't being nosey when asking about your cash flow; they're working with the intention of assessing whether you can afford to do what you plan to do. They may tell you to balance your budget if you're going backwards fast.

Positive cash flow is the *key* to any investment strategy, meaning that more cash is flowing into your money pool than what flows out of it. It's important to master your cash flow so you can start making powerful financial decisions.

Remember that budget I had you work on very early in the book? There was a very important reason for that

The budget exercise was the first step in measuring your future success. Income has to exceed expenditure so you can start to invest and create wealth for yourself. You always need positive cash flow to be successful.

Your assets

Assets include bank accounts, share investments, managed fund investments and property. Even valuable collectables such as art, wine and jewellery can be consider to be assets. This assists in determining the options at your disposal. It's also used to decide the level of protection required for your lifestyle and assets.

* * *

Many people don't understand that by spending some time, effort and money on getting the right, professional advice early, preferably before making an investment decision, it's possible to save yourself money and stress. Your chosen professional can provide the necessary advice or set you in the right direction of the information and/or services required.

Mind Your Money Tip

Be certain you're using money as effectively as possible.
Be prepared to recognise and act on opportunities.

Chapter 15

Conclusion

Wow you made it to the end—congratulations! I'm so glad you invested your time and emotional energy to get this far. My hope is you've added value to your future by understanding how to control your finances instead of letting them control you. I hope to have delivered nuggets of wisdom you can use.

I've worked with many hundreds of clients seeking specific advice on a one-on-one basis; all willing to pay for advice to ensure they transform their financial future. Yet others never have the chance to learn how to be smart with money; they coast along as their situation gets progressively worse. Because you've made it this far, *you're ready to transform your own financial future*, to break old habits and create a future to be proud of.

I've had clients say they thought I was being too tough only to thank me later for the tough love and straight shooting. Making a difference to the relationship people have with money is exciting and emotionally rewarding.

I'm keen to hear of your successes, so please share your success by emailing: info@prosperityplanning.com.au.

You now have some knowledge and are starting to develop your money muscles—it's time to start exercising! All muscles need exercise; keep taking steps towards being financially independent. As you exercise you will develop better financial judgement while gaining confidence to implement plans for the future.

Before you go, I'd like to remind you that your journey to financial mastery has only just begun. It's up to you to choose to re-write your future. Take time to map out the path you want to take. Create a basic outline, some 'chapter titles' if you will, then flesh out the content as you go.

If you're stuck or afraid of making a decision, ask what might happen if everything goes right as well as considering what might go wrong—look at both sides. Ask as many questions as you need to make a decision—just make a decision. It's important to move ahead and not remain stuck in the limbo of 'what if'. Decide if the 'thing' is worth the risk. If you can't decide, get professional assistance to help you decide if the risk is worth taking.

One last suggestion … Sit quietly and ask yourself what you truly want to achieve; make a list as ideas come to you. Trust your gut and write everything down, even if it sounds silly. The ideas could be your 'chapter titles', the start of your grand plan for how you rule your money and the start of your future successes.

Once results start happening, you'll notice the door to more opportunities will open, as if by magic. It's actually *you* that is allowing that flow to happen.

To your success and prosperity.

Gayle McKew

Know clearly what you want to achieve and let the Universe know!

How to work with Gayle McKew

Reading a book is well and good, but I always like learning by bouncing ideas off others. Sometimes people I speak with have absolutely no idea what I am talking about, which only serves to make me realise just how much I have learned. Engage and be inspired by future possibilities; be your financial best.

Life is a journey sweeping us through unexpected twists and turns, like divorces and unplanned changes of circumstances. There may be times when you find yourself 'stuck' or feeling at a loss as to which way to turn. I'm here to support your progress. I publish information/opinions/blog pieces on www.womenmindyourmoney.com.au that will help your money journey.

www.prosperityplanning.com.au focuses on financial planning in greater depth and will be useful as you develop your money muscles.

If you find you need a little more than a book to re-set your mindset and re-start your life, I recommend you check www.gaylemckew.com to find the most suitable emotional transformation methods for your needs. Here I offer coaching, retreats and workshops.

I'm available for personal advice by arrangement. This option is only for the truly committed person; one looking for a personal breakthrough in how they see and use money. Together we can tailor-make a strategy for your success.

Personal consultations can be arranged by contacting info@prosperityplanning.com.au. My intention is to inspire your financial success and prosperity on all levels. Enjoy the ride!

Gayle

Appendix 1

Create A Budget *Mind Your Money Activity 1*

Expense Items	Frequency*	Frequency Amount	Annualised Expense
Example: Food	52	$100	$5200
ESSENTIAL LIVING COSTS			
Food			
Personal care			
Child care			
Child maintenance			
Education			
Outings/Dining/etc.			
Miscellaneous			
	Sub-total		

LIFESTYLE EXPENDITURE			
Alcohol/Cigarettes			
Music/DVDs/Leisure			
Postage			
Recreational activities			
Raffles/Lotto/Pokies etc.			
Children's sport/activities			
Children's education			
Vacations			
Pay TV			
Clothing/Shoes/Apparel			
Gifts (Christmas/birthdays)			

Charities/Tithe			
Computing/Internet			
ATM withdrawals/ Pocket money			
	Sub-total		

TRANSPORT EXPENSES			
Registration/Insurance			
Fuel/Parking			
Servicing/Parts/Cleaning			
Bus/Train/taxi			
Miscellaneous			
	Sub-total		

EXTERNAL ADVICE AND PROFESSIONAL SERVICES			
Accounting fees			
Doctors (out of pocket/ gap only)			
Dentist (out of pocket/ gap only)			
Pharmacy (out of pocket/ gap only)			
Chiropractor (out of pocket/gap only)			
Physio (out of pocket/ gap only)			
Orthodontist (out of pocket/gap only)			
Optometrist (out of pocket/gap only)			

Masseuse (out of pocket/ gap only)			
Veterinarian			
	Sub-total		

INSURANCE EXPENSES			
Home/Contents			
Motor vehicle/Roadside			
Health fund (after rebate)			
Life/Trauma cover			
Income protection			
Ambulance cover			
Boat/Trailer/Caravan/ Pet insurance(s)			
	Sub-total		

BANKING FEES			
Account/Loan fees			
Miscellaneous fees			
Credit card fees (annual fee and interest costs)			
	Sub-total		

HOUSEHOLD UPKEEP			
Repairs/Renovations			
General upkeep/ Maintenance			
Furnishing			
	Sub-total		

INVESTMENT PROPERTY RELATED EXPENSES			
Insurance			
Rates			
Body corp.			
Maintenance			
Interest costs			
Other			
	Sub-total		

BUSINESS EXPENSES			
All business expenses			
	Sub-total		

OTHER MISCELLANEOUS			
Hairdresser/Beauty			
Memberships/ Subscriptions			
Credit cards			
Personal education costs			
Pet grooming			
	Sub-total		

Wealth Builders			
Savings			
Personal savings			
Emergency fund			
	Sub-total		

ESSENTIAL LIVING COSTS	**Sub-total**		
LIFESTYLE EXPENDITURE	**Sub-total**		
TRANSPORT EXPENSES	**Sub-total**		
EXTERNAL ADVICE AND PROFESSIONAL SERVICES	**Sub-total**		
INSURANCE EXPENSES	**Sub-total**		
BANKING FEES	**Sub-total**		
HOUSEHOLD UPKEEP	**Sub-total**		
INVESTMENT PROPERTY RELATED EXPENSES	**Sub-total**		
BUSINESS EXPENSES	**Sub-total**		
WEALTH BUILDERS	**Sub-total**		
OTHER MISCELLANEOUS	**Sub-total**		
	Total		

Income after tax (from wages or salary)^			
Other Income (from second job)			
	Sub-total		

Business Income (after costs including tax)			
Investment Income (after costs including tax)			
	Total		

^Generally this is the amount credited to your account each pay period or that you receive from your employer if you are paid in cash or by cheque.

Total income items			
Less			
Total expense items			
Total surplus/shortfall			
Surplus = Money available to create your future			

~ This will either be a positive or a negative figure. A negative figure means your costs currently exceed your total income.

Acknowledgements

Thank you from the bottom of my heart to all who have encouraged me to develop self-belief and to put pen to paper.

Understanding the knowledge I take for granted as an intrinsic part of myself was special, and learning to appreciate skills peculiar to me was a journey in itself entirely separate to the book. Realising money knowledge is not something everyone has had access to was an eye opener, finally allowing me to see I had something to offer to others.

It's been a huge leap of faith to transfer some of the knowledge accumulated in my head onto paper. There have been many words of encouragement and guidance from special people with more belief in me than I could ever imagine. Thank you from the bottom of my heart.

For Kim and Bronwyn; thanks for being my test pilots and reading the first horribly boring draft! You deserve medals. You also allowed me to see there was a need for something like this.

Dimity, Rhonda and Sonya; thank you for the inspiration for the title. I still can't get that song out of my head!

A huge thank you to Wendy Millgate of Wendy & Words; your guidance, tolerance and patience have been heaven-sent. No words can fully explain my gratitude.

To Ocean, the final part in the hippy cohort; thank you for your vision and support.

About the Author

Gayle McKew has a passion for money and personal empowerment. She believes money is meant to flow and to benefit all. Yet she knows many people lack the knowledge to work with flow effectively. We all deserve some of the financial abundance pie; many haven't had the opportunity to discover the mindset, knowledge and skills required to do so. Gayle had to learn too. She was on a money rollercoaster early in life, with lots of necessary learning curves.

Having gained many years of industry experience, Gayle eventually took a leap of faith to start a business. The result was her company, Prosperity Planning, a financial planning service that offers boutique, tailor-made financial solutions in the areas of retirement planning, superannuation, aged-care advice and estate planning. She hasn't looked back.

Gayle has always had her feet in two worlds: the financial world and the 'hippy' world. While she is trained in financial matters and knows superannuation and mortgages so well, she has also immersed herself in the world of energy, conscious creation, mindset, the environment and the laws of attraction. It's a unique situation to be able to offer clients practical tools and strategies, as well as spiritual principles and the keys to a successful mindset and values make-over, to ensure they're not repeating the same financial disasters.

After listening to friends' financial dilemmas and the disasters they were experiencing, the penny dropped. Gayle was amazed to discover how much essential financial information wasn't widely known. In fact, women were often the worst impacted, finding themselves ill-prepared financially. The biggest impact was from lack of information and opportunity, rather than a lack of ability. It was time to share her knowledge so others could benefit.

Gayle unpacked much of her wisdom in her latest book *Women Mind Your Money ... Before Someone Else Does.* It's certainly not everything she offers, yet it's a good start to help women make real working plans for managing future wealth.

Inspiring and empowering women to be the best version of themselves is part of what's driven Gayle to share. Helping set women up for personal success in all areas—life, money and relationships—is her passion.

Her skills extend to personal coaching and removing blocks that hold you back. Gayle can be contacted through www.gaylemckew.com and her Facebook page, Women of Wisdom, is providing an avenue to 'shift the stuff' that bothers or blocks the flow of abundance and joy in women's lives.

Gayle is happy to guide you through the financial maze and to provide clarity while removing confusion or blockages that are keeping you from financial success. It *is* possible to plan for prosperity. It all begins with learning how to mind your money.

Made in United States
North Haven, CT
07 November 2026

21928338R00124